Improving Competitiveness through Human Resource Development in China

This book looks at the development of vocational education and training in China and how it is crucial to human resource development and improving competitiveness. It briefly outlines the contextual issues related to vocational education and training in China, the importance of vocational education and how China has been using vocational training to reduce the unemployment rate and raise its overall human capital.

Min Min graduated from the School of Management at the University of South Australia. Her teaching and research interests include strategic HRM, human resource development (HRD), international HRM and comparative studies of HRM systems among emerging economies.

Ying Zhu is Professor and Director of the Australian Centre for Asian Business at the University of South Australia. Ying has published widely in the areas of international HRM, international business and economic development in Asia. Ying has published numerous articles and books.

Routledge Advances in Management and Business Studies

Women in Business Families
From Past to Present
Jarna Heinonen and Kirsi Vainio-Korhonen

Transformative Management Education
The Role of the Humanities and Social Sciences
Ulrike Landfester and Jörg Metelmann

Operating Under High-Risk Conditions in Temporary Organizations
A Sociotechnical Systems Perspective
Matthijs Moorkamp

Decision-making for New Product Development in Small Businesses
Mary Haropoulou and Clive Smallman

Frugal Innovation and the New Product Development Process
Insights from Indonesia
*Stephanie B.M. Cadeddu, Jerome D. Donovan, Cheree Topple,
Gerrit A. de Waal and Eryadi K. Masli*

Ethical Branding and Marketing
Cases and Lessons
Edited by Hagai Gringarten and Raúl Fernández-Calienes

Diversity and Entrepreneurship
Edited by Vanessa Ratten and Leo-Paul Dana

**Improving Competitiveness through Human Resource
Development in China**
The Role of Vocational Education
Min Min and Ying Zhu

For more information about this series, please visit www.routledge.com/Routledge-
Advances-in-Management-and-Business-Studies/book-series/SE0305

Improving Competitiveness through Human Resource Development in China

The Role of Vocational Education

Min Min and Ying Zhu

Routledge
Taylor & Francis Group

LONDON AND NEW YORK

First published 2020
by Routledge
2 Park Square, Milton Park, Abingdon, Oxon OX14 4RN

and by Routledge
52 Vanderbilt Avenue, New York, NY 10017

Routledge is an imprint of the Taylor & Francis Group, an informa business

First issued in paperback 2021

British Library Cataloguing-in-Publication Data
A catalogue record for this book is available from the British Library

Library of Congress Cataloging-in-Publication Data
A catalog record has been requested for this book

ISBN: 978-1-138-62510-5 (hbk)
ISBN: 978-1-03-208963-8 (pbk)
ISBN: 978-0-429-46019-7 (ebk)

Typeset in Galliard
by codeMantra

Contents

Figures

Tables

Acknowledgements

This project received substantial support from the Australian Centre for Asian Business at the University of South Australia.

We would like to thank Professor Chen Jiao in Fuzhou, China for her support in providing many valuable documents and historical record of VET schools' development in China. This book is dedicated to her contributions to the VET systems in China for more than three decades.

We would also like to thank Marina Morgan for her diligent work and help in the final proofreading. We are grateful for the assistance that we have received from the team at Routledge, Singapore, including Samantha Phua and Yongling Lam.

Finally, we would like to thank all the leaders at different VET schools in China for supporting our fieldworks there and providing valuable documents for preparing this book. Without their insights and candid thoughts, compiling this book would not have been conceivable.

May 2019
Min Min
Ying Zhu

1 Introduction

It has been 40 years since economic reform and opening-up was initiated in China. During this period, China's industrial structure has been upgraded, leading to a surge in service sectors and hi-tech industries. The traditional blue-collar industries declined across the country, being increasingly replaced by a skilled and professional workforce in the areas such as accounting, automotive, finance and marketing, hospitality, IT and telecommunications. As shown by the official data, tertiary industries accounted for 24.6% of GDP in 1978 but increased to 51.6% in 2018 (National Bureau of Statistics, 2018).

The wave of globalisation has given companies in emerging economies unprecedented opportunities to reach global markets, allowing them to 'leapfrog' decades of technological developments in the West. 'Path dependency' is less important than people assumed and emerging economies such as China are moving up the value chain, willing to 'raise their game'. Although China accounts for a steadily increasing share of world manufacturing, its low-cost competitive advantage is transitory and there is a growing tendency for China to move into high-skilled and high value-added production and services. This shift requires Chinese workers to have strong literacy, numeracy and problem-solving skills, skills in the use of technologies, social and emotional skills, and the capacity and motivation to learn and develop. Hence, there is a great demand for better education and training systems in China (Yao, 2019). Additionally, the prosperity of the nation is seen to rest on the skills, knowledge and enterprise of all individuals rather than on a few from the elite. Thus, the importance of investment in education at all levels has been emphasised. However, since skills development takes place outside the formal education system, particularly in vocational education, training institutions and within corporations, concerted efforts from the government, vocational institutions and private sectors are needed.

In China, all citizens must attend school for at least nine years, including six years of primary school and three years of lower secondary school, known as the 'nine-year compulsory education' (Zhu & Warner, 2013). Students can then choose to continue their study in upper secondary school for another three years, attend secondary vocational schools or enter the labour market. In this book, we want to focus on the students who attend secondary vocational schools. It is noteworthy that in 2017, over 7,490,000 students graduated from universities and the number for 2019 is estimated to be around 8,350,000. Although most were able to find jobs (91.6% in 2017), only 77.1% found full-time employment. As for vocational students, 92.1% of tertiary vocational graduates (3,516,448 graduates in 2017) and 96.7% of secondary vocational graduates (4,968,770 graduates in 2017) found full-time jobs (MyCOS, 2018). This is the first time that the percentage of vocational students exceeds that of university graduates in terms of obtaining full-time employment. The implication may be that enrolment in higher education (i.e. universities) is no longer an assurance of a job, given the more favourable employment rate of secondary vocational students.

Vocational education in China

Generally speaking, vocational education in China is provided at three levels: lower secondary, upper secondary and tertiary. Lower secondary vocational school is rare and mostly provided in remote regions. Upper secondary schools account for the major part of the Chinese vocational education system. There are 10,671 upper secondary vocational schools with 15,924,968 students and 1,388 tertiary vocational schools with 11,049,549 students (Ministry of Education of the People's Republic of China, 2018). In terms of the number of students, the differences between secondary vocational schools and tertiary vocational schools do not appear significant (approx. 4,000,000 more in secondary vocational schools). However, the regional coverage of the secondary vocational schools is much wider because the Chinese government requires that each county has at least one secondary vocational school. Furthermore, during the four decades of reform and opening-up, China has experienced the largest and fastest urbanisation in the world. This rapid urbanisation would not have been possible without the help of a large workforce, mostly from rural areas. With the transformation to an urban society, people from rural areas need to be trained in order to obtain jobs in the urban areas. Considering the educational background of rural people, secondary vocational schools are more suitable and prepare them for such a 'transformation' (Yi et al., 2015). Additionally, providing opportunities for the disadvantaged population has become one of the major social development issues in China. Secondary vocational schools act as a means of inclusion, giving certain disadvantaged groups, such as those from poverty-stricken families and those with disabilities, access to schooling and job opportunities in the labour market. For these disadvantaged students, the system is an attractive plan as they receive exemption of tuition fees and can enter the labour market earlier than tertiary vocational students, who must spend three years in upper high schools and then three to four years in tertiary vocational schools.

Since initiating economic reform in 1978, China has had a remarkable period of rapid growth shifting from a centrally planned to a market-oriented economy and has experienced rapid economic and social development. The GDP growth has averaged nearly 10% a year, the fastest sustained expansion by a major economy in history and has lifted more than 800 million people out of poverty. Although China's GDP growth has gradually slowed since 2012, it is still impressive by current global standards. In 2017, its GDP reached approximately 12.238 trillion, with a growth of 6.9% in comparison to 2.3% in the United States (The World Bank Group, 2017).

With regard to the total workforce on the supply side, China's working-age population (15–59 years old) peaked at 925,000,000 in 2011 and has fallen every year since then, with a drop of 3,450,000 in 2012, 2,440,000 in 2013, 3,710,000 in 2014, and 4,870,000 in 2015. According to an estimate by the Ministry of Human Resources and Social Security, the working-age population is expected to see a sharp drop from 830 million in 2030 to 700 million in 2050 at a declining rate of 7,600,000 every year (National Bureau of Statistics, 2018).

With a shrinking workforce, labour costs increase. For a long time, the workforce in China entered the job market with a low educational background (i.e. lower secondary graduates or below) and became low-cost labour for the manufacturing industry. Today, university enrolments are increasing and fundamentally changing the quality and structure of the workforce since university graduates account for half of the newly increased workforce. Though the educational background of the workforce is being enhanced, the skill sets typically do not match market demand. This mismatch is illustrated in Tables 1.1 and 1.2, using data from Beijing, Anhui and Guangxi, which represent northern, central and southwestern areas respectively.

From these tables, it is obvious that the majority of current students are majoring in tertiary industries (81.22% in Beijing, 71.37% in Anhui and 66.86% in Guangxi). The figures are higher than the percentage contributed by tertiary industries to overall GDP (51.6% in China). In loose terms, these figures may indicate that the skills nurtured in schools do not translate proportionally into productivity. This low efficiency of transformation may be caused by a number of factors, one of which may be the programmes and courses determined by educational institutions without proper consideration of market demand. A detailed analysis of this aspect will be presented in the following chapters.

In addition, the turnover rate among young employees is high, with about one-third of graduates leaving their jobs within six months of graduation (MyCOS, 2018). Some of the graduates do not have clear plans for their careers and have unrealistic expectations of new jobs. Chasing higher salaries and better working conditions are two of the major reasons for young people shifting jobs.

Table 1.1 GDP and GDP of primary, secondary, and tertiary industries (hundred million RMB)

	Beijing	Anhui	Guangxi
GDP	19,500.60	19,038.87	14,378.00
GDP of primary industry	161.80	2,348.09	2,343.57
GDP of secondary industry	4,352.80	10,403.96	6,863.04
GDP of tertiary industry	14,986.50	6,282.82	5,171.39

Source: China Vocational Education Yearbook (2015).

Table 1.2 Number of current students in secondary vocational schools

	Beijing	Anhui	Guangxi
Majors in primary industry	1,704	5,733	5,948
Majors in secondary industry	18,627	128,528	97,918
Majors in tertiary industry	87,982	334,773	209,561
Total	108,313	469,034	313,427

Source: China Vocational Education Yearbook (2015).

Furthermore, although the government is increasing its subsidies to vocational education, its spending has long favoured general education over vocational education and training. Government spending per university student is around three times that spent on a tertiary vocational student. Subsidies for secondary vocational students are even less, thus affecting the education quality of vocational schools, especially secondary schools (Ministry of Education of the People's Republic of China, 2018).

On the demand side, it must first be noted that China is transitioning from being the 'world's factory' for low-end products to becoming a provider of high-end manufacturing and services. This has led to a greater demand for labour with upgraded skills and competence. Data from the Ministry of Human Resources and Social Security (2016) shows that skilled workers account for only about 19% of the entire workforce, with highly skilled workers constituting only 5%.

Second, although the manufacturing sector continues to be the main pillar of the Chinese economy as mentioned above, tertiary industries, especially modern services that deal with IT, software, accounting, marketing and customer management, are expected to grow in the foreseeable future and will need a substantial number of skilled employees and professionals.

Third, due to geographical and historical reasons, the eastern provinces of China enjoy a higher level of economic development than inland provinces and attract a larger pool of highly skilled workers, leading to an agglomeration of high value-added industries in these eastern provinces (Zhang & Rasiah, 2015). Due to the increased cost of land and labour and high-profit margins, these high value-added industries force out low value-added industries which consequently must relocate to inland provinces or neighbouring countries. Such an uneven development of industries leads to differing regional demands in terms of skilled workforce. In addition to the disparities in regional demand for highly skilled workers within the same industry, skills shortages vary across different company ownerships and sizes. In general, domestic private companies suffer severer shortages than foreign companies. Small- and medium-sized companies tend to experience intense skills shortages compared with larger ones.

It appears that China's economy is robust and human capital is growing. However, the economic transformation and structural changes have resulted in increased skills shortages and mismatches. Demand and supply are dangerously skewed. Low-skilled workers are not ready for highly skilled and high value-added production, while the skills obtained through previous work and training are not those needed by new industries. Vocational education and training play a critical role in closing this skills gap and mismatch, thus justifying a detailed investigation.

Urbanisation and migrant workers

Urbanisation is one of the key strategies adopted by the Chinese government to boost domestic demand. During the process of urbanisation, China has been expanding its cities rapidly and building new urbanised centres in rural regions with the intention of modernising its countryside and narrowing income disparities. By the end of 2017, the number of China's permanent urban population had reached 813,470,000, accounting for 58.52% of the total population. Since 2012, 101,650,000 rural people have become permanent urban residents (National Bureau of Statistics, 2018). Workforce supply appears to be abundant, however, a small proportion of the increased urban population can be counted as skilled workers.

In rural areas, the changed incentive mechanism and introduction of technology have drastically increased agricultural labour productivity, leading to a surplus agricultural workforce and the transfer of this workforce into urban industrial production. Furthermore, with the abolition of communes and the improved '*hukou*' system, namely the household registration system, people can move to and live in urban areas without restriction (Griffiths & Schiavone, 2016). However, the problem confronting migrant workers has been the preparation for jobs in urban areas. In fact, in China, the quality of education in rural areas is significantly lower than that in urban areas. The first generation of workers from rural areas is employed mostly in the manufacturing and construction industries as non-skilled or semi-skilled workers. Not only do these workers have low-income levels and little social security, they also have restricted access to formal skills training at the workplace, thus reducing their chance of upward mobility. Although the younger generation of migrant workers is better educated than their parents, skills levels are still relatively low and job-training opportunities at the workplace are rare. Therefore, vocational schools, especially secondary vocational schools, are a pragmatic instrument to improve the skills of the migrant urban workforce.

In addition to migrant urban workers, there are other socially vulnerable and disadvantaged groups, such as people from families below the poverty line. Once the nine-year compulsory education has been completed, the tuition fee for upper secondary schools is a heavy financial burden, although secondary vocational school tuition fees are free. When choosing between working in labour-intensive industries and studying at secondary vocational schools to obtain particular skills, most young people are choosing the second option.

Key research questions and the structure of the book

We have briefly described the vocational education system, the current status of the workforce, the problem of the skills shortage and the need for skills development in China. In order to further elaborate those issues and challenges in this book, we have established the following key research questions as the central theme for a detailed investigation: (1) What is the history of Vocational Education and Training (VET) in China? (2) What are the policy initiatives on VET in China? (3) What is the process of VET development in responding to the ongoing challenges for skills development in China? (4) How do training and career development facilitate the development of teaching staff in secondary vocational schools in China? (5) To what extent does VET facilitate the increase of employer satisfaction and student career development?

In order to understand the Chinese VET system, the first key area we intend to review is the system's history, an area in which limited study has been conducted. In China, vocational schools are a part of public education, being planned, built and managed by the government as well as receiving subsidies from the government. Since the sector is heavily reliant on the government, a study of government's policies and their effects on vocational schools and the VET system is meaningful. Given the importance of VET, what policies are implemented and whether there are opportunities for the government to make improvements form the second key question we wish to answer. Furthermore, the development of VET requires joint efforts by the government, industrial partners, teachers and students. This book, therefore, explores options for improving the overall development of the VET system, vocational teachers' skills, employer satisfaction and student career development.

In order to address these key questions, this book elaborates the relevant issues from a historical perspective with the guidance of underpinning literature. Therefore, Chapter 2 focuses on the existing human resources development (HRD) literature and subsequently, shifts the focus to the literature on vocational education and training. The chapter provides an overview of different VET systems across different countries such as Germany, Japan and the United Kingdom. This international comparative analysis will allow us to identify the position of China's HRD in general, and the VET system in particular, within the international arena.

Chapter 3 provides an overview of the history and policy of vocational education in China. First, we review the history of vocational education, which can be traced back to the Qing dynasty, indicating that vocational education has been embedded in the Chinese education system for a long time and has evolved with the introduction of Western concepts. In China, vocational education is also influenced by policy and culture, which provide context to our study. Education policy has been undergoing a great transformation in China. The economic reform and the pursuit of rapid economic growth have significantly impacted Chinese VET and its development. With regard to cultural issues, few studies have considered this aspect and have mainly done so in terms of critiquing the negative impact of Confucianism on vocational education as it values theoretical knowledge and accords lower status and value to VET. However, culture should be considered an important factor in shaping social action and behaviour as well as producing an ingrained understanding of the world. Thus, exploration of the cultural dimension is necessary for us to understand how VET in China has been shaped, developed and transformed. By bringing historical, political and cultural issues into our study, we are able to draw a relatively comprehensive picture of vocational education in China.

Chapter 4 continues to explore the evolution and current status of VET in China, using a number of cases which cover different regions and different industries in China. In an ever-changing economy, characterised by the introduction of new technologies, the collapsing of barriers to international trade, and the tendency of moving from low value-added to high value-added products, a greater number of skilled workers is required in the workplace. Despite boasting the world's largest workforce, the lack of skills experienced by the country's industries stands as the most challenging issue in national development plans. Chinese companies are failing to find the highly skilled employees they need, while people find themselves ill-prepared for the jobs that are available. In the light of such an acute skills shortage, we describe the efforts which have been made by VET schools to increase the quality of the workforce, to smooth young people's transition from school to the workplace and to speed up transformation and transfer skills to where they are needed most. In more details, this chapter also provides information and analysis on the reform of school management, approaches to teaching and curriculum, and upgrade of skills and knowledge among teaching staff through on-the-job training and off-the-job training, as well as management of teaching staff career development through adequate HRD policies and practices. The chapter also draws attention to the outcomes of VET development, namely satisfaction with employer and student career development. It is understandable that vocational education has long held a lower status compared to general education in China. However, the students from vocational schools who may not excel academically, may be skilful at other occupations that remain indispensable to economic development and social prosperity. Therefore, enhancing employer satisfaction in skills matching and student career satisfaction is meaningful as it can help develop business and student self-esteem, as well as make contributions to national production potentials and further economic development.

Chapter 5 summarises and analyses findings from our literature review, describes case studies and interviews, and discusses what is meant by contemporary vocational education and the relevant HRD issues in China. By integrating information collected from governing bodies, employers, teachers and students, we hope to provide multiple perspectives on HRD and vocational education and enrich understanding of these themes which are expected to have useful implications for practitioners, scholars and policymakers.

Concluding remarks

China is reforming its economy so as to adapt to the challenges of globalisation. Reforming and developing the VET system is crucial for China's future competitiveness given the globalisation process has accelerated competition among nations. So far, considerable progress has been achieved by China, as reflected in the significant rise in economic growth and productivity. Within such a context, globalisation further challenges VET in how it fulfils its role in developing people's relevant competencies for their effective and efficient performance within the world of work, and in sustaining those competencies in the long term.

The VET system in China was established during a movement of self-strengthening. With the founding of the People's Republic of China, the country borrowed the VET system from the Soviet Union and then introduced other systems, such as those practised in Germany, Japan and Britain, in order to cope with rapid changes and challenges brought by globalisation. For the time being, it appears that China continues to experiment with its VET system in an attempt to find ways to adjust to rapidly changing social and economic environments while remaining connected to its cultural and spiritual roots.

References

China Vocational Education Yearbook, 2015. Beijing: Economy and Management Publishing House.

Griffiths, M. and Schiavone, M., 2016. China's new urbanisation plan 2014–20. *China Report*, 52(2), pp. 73–91.

Ministry of Education of People's Republic of China, 2018. [online] http://www.moe.gov.cn/s78/A03/ Available at: http://www.moe.gov.cn/s78/A03/moe_560/jytjsj_2017/qg/201808/t20180808_344698.htm [accessed on 16 January 2019]

Ministry of Human Resources and Social Security, 2016. [online] http://www.mohrss.gov.cn Available at http://www.mohrss.gov.cn/SYrlzyhshbzb/zwgk/szrs/ndtjsj/ [accessed on 16 January 2019]

MyCOS, 2018. *Chinese 4-year college graduates' employment annual report.* Beijing: Social Sciences Academic Press.

National Bureau of Statistics, 2018. [online] http://www.stats.gov.cn Available at: http://www.stats.gov.cn/tjsj/zxfb/201802/t20180228_1585631.html [accessed on 17 January 2019]

The World Bank Group, 2017. [online] https://www.worldbank.org Available at: https://www.worldbank.org/en/country/china [accessed on 16 January 2019]

Yao, Y., 2019. Does higher education expansion enhance productivity? *Journal of Macroeconomics*, 59, pp. 169–194.

Yi, H., Zhang, L., Yao, Y., Wang, A., Ma, Y., Shi, Y., Chu, J., Loyalka, P. and Rozelle, S., 2015. Exploring the dropout rates and causes of dropout in upper-secondary technical and vocational education and training (TVET) schools in China. *International Journal of Educational Development*, 42, pp. 115–123.

Zhang, M. and Rasiah, R., 2015. Globalization, industrialization and labour markets in China. *Journal of the Asia Pacific Economy*, 20(1), pp. 14–41.

Zhu, Y. and Warner, M. 2013. Workforce development and skill formation in China: A new 'long march', in J. Benson, H. Gospel and Y. Zhu (eds.), *Workforce Development and Skill Formation in Asia*. London and New York: Routledge, pp. 142–158.

2 Conceptual issues and background

The human capital construct is the central focus of this book. It is widely recognised that human capital is an important asset and one of the key drivers of corporate success and sustained comparative advantage (Barney & Wright, 1998). Therefore, the relevant literature on human capital as well as the key concepts related to Human Resource Development (HRD) and VET comprise the major part of this chapter. Following a review of the foundation issues related to the key conceptual issues, the focus of this chapter shifts to different VET systems and operations among a number of key countries, including Germany, the UK and Japan, that have significantly influenced the Chinese VET system and reform. Finally, this chapter will describe the background of the Chinese VET system, its evolution in the country's history and its reform in more recent years.

Human capital and HRD

Generally speaking, human capital is defined as employees' explicit and implicit knowledge and abilities, which lead to organisational competitiveness (Schultz, 1960). Although there are considerable disagreements about the definition, the core characteristics of human capital include knowledge, skills, abilities and other characteristics (KSAOs) embodied in individuals (Coff, 2002). To be specific, 'knowledge' is the factual or procedural information necessary for performing a specific job and the foundation on which skills and abilities are developed; 'skills' are the individual's level of proficiency and capabilities to perform a specific job task; 'ability' is a more enduring capability (usually cognitive) that is necessary for an individual to perform a job; and 'other characteristics' often refer to personality traits or other attributes that affect the individual's ability to perform a specific job (Knowles, Holton III & Swanson, 2012). Besides these widely recognised core characteristics, other traits exist which could be considered valuable such as loyalty, the need for achievement and social capital. These traits may expand the boundaries of human capital and raise questions as to how to cultivate these traits.

Given the importance of human capital, how to acquire, train and develop it becomes critical and has been discussed across different disciplines such as psychology, human resources management and human resources development.

Within the realm of human resources management at the organisational level, the acquirement of human capital largely relies on recruitment, typically on-campus recruiting which is beneficial to companies because it is an efficient way to meet a large number of students in a short time. On-campus recruiting gives companies a wide choice of candidates and builds links with the next cohort of students. In addition, new graduates tend to work closely with their first employer. Students know they can be offered a good job even before they complete their studies, thus smoothing their transition into the workplace. However, on-campus recruitment can be expensive and can lead to extra expenses such as travelling and training for new graduates who have had little practical job exposure.

After employees are recruited, training and development become essential to improve the human capital portfolio as well as to meet the specific requirements at the workplace – these aspects can be seen as a central element in organisations' HRD strategy. HRD was introduced in the 1960s and defined as the process of increasing the KSAOs of individuals (Harbison & Myers, 1964). The definition implies that the primary focus of HRD is the improvement of individuals. HRD has gradually evolved into a holistic process encompassing organisational learning and development as well as individual learning (Ruona, 1998). Methods utilised in HRD studies to cultivate employees' KSAOs fall into categories such as formal programmes, relationship-based developmental experiences and job-based developmental experiences (Conger, Conger & Martin, 2010).

Formal development programmes cover a broad spectrum of programmes including conceptual and skill-based development programmes, personal growth development programmes, feedback-based development interventions and action-focused development interventions (Conger, Conger & Martin, 2010). The majority of formal programmes are designed to enhance generic skills and behaviours such as teamwork, problem-solving and strategic awareness. The relationship-based developmental method is based on the assumption that relationships are increasingly central to the development process of KSAOs (Rock & Garavan, 2006). Individuals tend to have a developmental orientation. Being involved in developmental relationships in which an individual takes an active interest, is beneficial to individuals and eventually to organisations (Higgins & Kram, 2001). Employees are provided with a variety of developmental opportunities such as sponsorship, coaching, mentoring, psycho-social support and career advice. However, since developmental relationships commonly target high-potential employees (Garavan, Carbery & Rock, 2012), it presents significant challenges for organisations, such as finding the appropriate number of individuals who can perform roles as coaches and mentors, and addressing specific gender issues when matching mentors and mentees. Job-based development is based on the assumption that a job represents a primary source of development and can be used as the basis for KSAO development. Job-based development can provide five significant developmental opportunities: bosses and superiors, turnaround situations, increases in job scope, horizontal job moves and new initiatives such as doing a stretch task, implementing change and developing new practices (Wilson, 2011). By participating, employees are able to interact with the work context as part of their experience for KSAO development.

Most HRD literature emphasises formal development, however, it is important to challenge conventional thinking (Raelin, 1988), such as informal, incidental and implied developments. Informal development is unplanned with no specified outcomes, which is predominantly experiential. Incidental development is unintentional, a by-product of another activity and can be seen as a sub-category of informal learning (Marsick & Watkins, 2001). Implicit development is also part of learning, occurring independently from conscious attempts to learn, namely learning without awareness or explicit knowledge (Eraut, 2004). In this sense, non-formal learning is structured in terms of learning outcomes and it is considered to be an intentional development (Colley, Hodkinson & Malcolm, 2002). With the increasing emphasis on collective learning processes, non-formal training and development processes will be more frequently used and researched (Wang-Cowham, 2011).

Individuals rely on HRD activities to improve their current KSAOs and learn future KSAOs. Organisations rely on HRD to enhance the productivity and performance of their employees which is likely to enhance organisational competitiveness and sustainability (Mathieu, Tannenbaum & Salas, 1992). HRD is purposeful, planned, deliberate and involves the acquisition of key KSAOs (Wilson, 2012). A number of empirical studies have examined the relationship between HRD and performance. For example, one key element of HRD, namely extensive training, is positively related to increased productivity and minimised turnover intention (Aragon & Valle, 2013). Other HRD activities, such as coaching and mentoring, improve the exchange of collective knowledge which leads to job performance improvement (Liu & Batt, 2010). Other similar studies (Birdi et al., 2008, Frey, 2001, Klein & Weaver, 2000) also support the positive relationship between HRD and performance.

In this section, the discussion focuses on human capital and how to acquire, train and develop it via HRD in the workplace. Besides training and development, HRD is also closely related to education because students can be perceived as potential human capital to organisations. Education has the potential to enrich and provide students with opportunities for training and development as well as prepare them for work.

Vocational education and training

As stated above, training and development constitute a major part of HRD, while education is also an important aspect of HRD (Becker, DeGroot & Marschak, 1964). People receive 'education' within a compulsory schooling system and continue their further education, mixed with 'training', which prepares them for a particular job or profession. They then find a job and undergo 'training' and 'development' for a future career. In this sense, education, training and development have different focuses for enhancing human capital.

Most economies are concerned about the ease with which young workers can make the transition from school to work. Essentially, it is about minimising differences between KSAOs embodied in young workers and KSAOs needed at work. The smaller the differences, the easier the transition. In today's workplaces, employers want their employees to remain highly skilled and employable, targeting training and development activities within organisations, and seeking new employees with suitable employability. Meanwhile, many young workers struggle to find their place in the job market, changing jobs and occupations frequently before they settle down in a particular job with a sense of stability. Different schooling structures, vocational education and general education differ fundamentally in their focus on job transition. The general-vocational education debate has centred on whether vocational education is effective in facilitating youth school-to-work transition. Vocational education develops specific job-related skills in order to prepare students to work in specific occupations, while general education provides students with broad knowledge and basic skills such as mathematics and communication, and serves as the foundation for further learning and on-the-job training. These different perspectives suggest a possible trade-off between short-term and long-term costs and benefits for both individuals and the entire society. The skills generated by vocational education may facilitate the transition into the labour market quickly but may become obsolete at a faster rate (Paul, 2001). Although young employees encounter difficulties in adapting to technological and structural change in the economy, students' choices of VET are heavily based on short-term considerations and they tend to take an optimistic view of their future (Kreitzer & Klatt, 2017). Therefore, in terms of a smooth entry into the labour market by graduates, the advantages offered by VET are significant.

Vocational students are generally involved in two learning environments: a school offering theoretical knowledge and a workplace which is considered to be a place for practical skills. Viewed in the context of transition from school to the workplace, schooling provides formal theoretical institutional learning, while training at the workplace is career-based and does not comprise theoretical institutional learning. In various VET models, institutional learning and work-based training are combined in different proportions. In some countries such as the UK, VET focuses on formal apprenticeships with institutional instruction complementing workplace training. In other countries, such as Germany, a dual system is adopted with school-based and accredited training, with the elements of high degree formalisation and strong involvement of social partners. In China, vocational schools are a part of upper secondary education, although the focus is on practical skills. The curriculum adopted in vocational schools allocates a lower weight to general knowledge in comparison to general educational institutions. A more detailed comparison of different VET models will be presented in the next section.

VET is also an important place in which young people can form their identity during the transition from school to work (Jorgensen, 2013). VET provides students with in-depth vocational knowledge and rich opportunities to use the skills learned at school in a workplace context. Students thus progress towards being skilled members of the community of practitioners (Jorgensen, 2013). In addition, vocational qualifications improve students' employment chances (McIntosh, 2004, Karmel & Nguyen, 2006) and salary returns (Eichhorst,

Rodriguez-Plannas, Schmidl & Zimmermann, 2015). From a long-term perspective, once they have entered the labour market, graduates with VET qualifications achieve better full-time employment outcomes (Ryan, 2001), foster subsequent employment quality (Koen, Klehe, Van Vianen, Zikic & Nauta, 2010) and career success (Hirschi, 2010) than those without vocational qualifications.

Although VET is perceived to be one of the ways of enhancing a successful school-to-work transition and self-confidence, potential shortcomings and problems have been raised. For example, in terms of curriculum setting, it remains questionable whether the curriculum should be of interest to students or valuable to the labour market (Gerrard et al., 2013). In addition, albeit that vocational students learn the tools, techniques and routines of practices in a particular field, the question remains as to whether they would need to acquire conceptual knowledge as the base for these tools and techniques. Given an unpredictable and fast-changing labour market, how would vocational students adapt their past skills to the new work? Therefore, there is an urgent need to advance the VET model of learning and teaching in order to find new ways of thinking about combining the conceptual and practical knowledge and skills in supporting the development of a skilled workforce (Billett, 2015). Consequently, we need to consider different VET models across different countries to address these concerns.

VET systems across different countries

VET models differ globally and in some countries, especially in Europe, the concept of 'Big VET' has been adopted. This VET system includes school-based VET courses, workplace training, on-the-job training and training for promotion, transfer and re-employment. In China, the VET model is more traditional and 'small', meaning school-based VET, but not beyond. With the influence of other countries such as Germany, the UK and Japan, China's VET system has been evolving and reforming in more recent years. Incentives are being created for employers to participate in VET, thus addressing the poor public perception of VET, building bridges between vocational education and academic education, and redesigning the vocational education curriculum by combining conceptual and practical knowledge and skills.

German VET system

Germany is one of the largest countries in Europe, facing a number of challenges such as the ongoing refugee crisis and the European sovereign debt crisis as well as its aging population. In terms of total numbers of refugees, no other country in the European Union has been impacted as much by the current wave of refugees as Germany. According to the Ministry of the Interior, in 2015 the country accepted 890,000 refugees and received 476,649 formal applications for political asylum – the highest annual number of applications in the history of the Federal Republic (Federal Statistical Office of Germany, 2016). Integrating such large numbers of migrants, half of whom are below the age of 25, is a challenge for Germany, and access to education is a vital and feasible solution. Germany has the world's second oldest population after Japan, with 28% of its citizens aged 60 years or over. The Federal Statistical Office of Germany estimated that the population will decline from 82.1 million in 2015 to 67.6 million people by 2060 (Federal Statistical Office of Germany, 2016). This drop could undermine the government's ability to fund public services and weaken the country's economic foundations.

Compulsory education in Germany starts at age six, and in most states lasts for nine years. Elementary education is the only stage in German education where all students study at the same type of school. From Grades 1 to 4 (Grades 1 to 6 in some states), almost all German students attend *Grundschule* (foundation school), where they study the same basic general subjects. At the end of this foundation cycle, students move on to different types of lower secondary schools, based on their academic ability. Parents can choose to send their children to secondary schools in the vocational stream or to enrol them in university-preparatory schools.

Lower secondary education along the vocational stream imparts basic general education and prepares students for entry into upper secondary vocational programmes. The two most common school types in this stream are the *Hauptschule* (general school, open to all students) and the more popular *Realschule* (a type of intermediate secondary school which requires good marks to enter). *Hauptschule* programmes usually end after Grade 9 and conclude with the award of the *Zeugnis des Hauptschulabschlusses* (certificate of completion of *Hauptschule*). Programmes offered at the *Realschule* are academically more demanding and last until Grade 10. Students graduate with the *Zeugnis des Realschulabschlusses* (certificate of completion of *Realschule*), sometimes also called *Mittlere Reife* (intermediate maturity). This certificate gives access to a wider range of vocational programmes and also allows for access to university-preparatory upper secondary education.

At the upper secondary level, Germany has a variety of different vocational programmes. One subset of these programmes is similar to programmes in the general academic stream in that students receive full-time classroom instruction. However, the most common form of secondary vocational education has a heavy focus on practical training. More than 50% of German vocational students learn in a work-based education system. This work-based vocational education system combines theoretical classroom instruction with practical training embedded in a real-life work environment. This system is often viewed as a model for other nations seeking to address high rates of unemployment, particularly among the youth. Students in this system are admitted upon completion of lower secondary education. The system is characterised by 'sandwich programs' in which students attend a vocational school on a part-time basis, either in coherent blocks of weeks, or for one or two days each week. The rest of the students' time is devoted to practical training at a workplace (Report on Vocational Education and Training, 2018). Companies participating in these programmes are obligated to provide training in accordance with national regulations and to pay students a modest salary. The programmes last two to three-and-a-half years and conclude with a final examination conducted by the responsible authority in the field, often regional industry associations like Chambers of Industry and Commerce and Chambers of Crafts. The final credential awarded to graduates is typically a formal, government-recognised qualification certifying students' skills in regulated vocations. Many vocational schools also offer students a pathway to tertiary education via double qualification courses. Students who take this pathway earn a *Zeugnis der Fachhochschulreife* (university of applied sciences maturity certificate), which qualifies them for access to a subset of higher education institutions, the universities of applied sciences, as well as regular universities in a small number of states. The theoretical part of this programme is commonly completed after 12 years (Federal Ministry of Education and Research, 2018).

Within the German high-quality VET system, the dual system can be considered to be a successful model of the smooth school-to-work transition. It is a system where enterprises cooperate with public-funded vocational schools. Rather than a loose agreement of cooperation between companies and schools, the cooperation in the German VET system is regulated by law. The Vocational Training Act of 1969, which was amended in 2005, introduced this close alliance between the Federal Government, the federal states and companies with a view to providing young people with training in nationally recognised occupations which is then documented accordingly by means of a certificate issued by a competent body such as a Chamber of Industry and Commerce (Müller-Jentsch, 2018). As a result, the law makes the companies or employers responsible for updating and creating new training regulations and occupational profiles. It further leads to standardised training, testing and certificates in all industries throughout Germany. Every student must study from the same textbooks and be familiar with the same tools, which ensure that all vocational students receive the same training regardless of region and company. Employers trust these certificates as evidence of what an individual knows and is able to do. In addition, since employers take part in the dual training scheme, they save recruitment costs and avoid the risk of hiring the wrong employee for the job. Students spend a few days a week at school learning foundation skills, such as mathematics and language, as well as the theory underpinning their work and the rest of their time is spent mainly in the workplace. The balance means students can receive market-relevant training that improves their chances in the labour market which is constantly evolving and requiring upgraded skills in response to the latest innovations. After three years of modestly paid work and study, most students join their training company, thus saving time searching for a job as well as smoothing their transition into the workplace.

Vocational training exists in many countries, but such schemes are rarely as popular as those in Germany. Over 50% of Germans enter the dual VET system as a pathway into employment. More young people follow VET programmes than go to university, even though many are qualified for further study.

VET system in the United Kingdom

The United Kingdom (UK) is a union of Great Britain (England, Scotland and Wales) and Northern Ireland. It has a market-based economy and is a major international trading power. Financial services as well as pharmaceutical, petroleum, automotive, aerospace, telecommunications and other technological industries play an important role in the country's economy, with the services industry being the largest contributor. Its population is currently 66.02 million (Office for National Statistics, 2017), having risen from just over 60 million in 2005, and its workforce (aged between 16 and 64 years old) stood at 31.7 million in 2016 (74.4% employment rate).

Similar to other countries in Europe, the UK labour market is demand-led, and a skills shortage is widespread in sectors such as medicine, health, social work, science and secondary education teaching. While a number of occupations will continue to exist for unskilled and low-skilled employees, more and higher paid jobs will increasingly require an intermediate level of skills and qualifications. For the first time, in 2012 there were more jobs requiring higher education degrees than jobs requiring low or no qualification. Therefore, it is becoming more important for people who want to work in the UK to possess specialist skills and attend higher education.

VET programmes in the UK range from initial introductory VET courses in upper secondary schools and colleges to programmes at a higher education level. Courses are offered in the shape of school-based programmes which combine general academic study with vocational components, broad vocational programmes and specialist occupational programmes that take place in a school or college setting and the workplace. Among these courses and programmes, those provided within schools have been described as 'weak vocational courses' with low participation rates. A range of 'stronger vocational courses' leading to qualifications are available outside the school system.

The UK qualifications framework is based on a systemic level of qualification, enabling employees to have their skills certified. In the past, many individuals did not have the opportunity to have their expertise formally validated. Such recognition has an empowering and motivating effect, giving people the confidence to raise their aspirations and pursue further and higher-level qualifications (National Institute of Adult Continuing Education, 2013).

According to the UK qualification system, the first certificate needed is the General Certificate of Secondary Education (GCSE). Studies for GCSE examinations generally take place over a period of two or three academic years, starting in Year 9 or Year 10 (at the age of around 14–15) for the majority of students, with examinations being set at the end of Year 11 (around the age of 16). The GCSE covers a range of academic subjects such as history and mathematics, and vocational subjects such as health, business and social care. Students who decide to leave school without pursuing further academic study towards qualifications such as university degrees, need to attain the General Certificate of Secondary Education (GCSE) in vocational subjects (Ofqual, 2018).

Formal VET in the UK is organised and developed within several national qualification frameworks. It has come a long way since the introduction of National Vocational Qualifications (NVQs) in 1986, evolving into the Qualification and Credit Framework (QCF) in 2008 and the Regulated Qualifications Framework (RQF) in 2015 which serves a central mechanism. The NVQs were skills-based awards that tested students' abilities to complete a job to a certain required standard. NVQs included a statement of competence and associated performance criteria relevant to the work. These work performance criteria were further grouped into units of competence. NVQs could be awarded on the basis of certain combinations of units and allowed for the accumulation of competencies with flexible time frames. The accumulation of competencies increased flexibility as well as employability as students or employees could choose to obtain the skills and certificate to fulfil immediate requirements at work. NVQs are a perfect example of the inherent skills-based approach in the UK (Ryan, Gospel & Lewis, 2006). However, the NVQs did not include the notion of competence development based on the integration of theoretical and practical knowledge, but instead focused on the performance of narrow tasks prescribed by employers.

In 2008, the Qualifications and Credit Framework (QCF) replaced NVQs, with the intention of bringing vocational and academic qualifications together in one framework (QCDA, 2010). The system requires students to earn credits. One credit usually takes around ten hours to complete. These credits build up to form full qualifications. There are three different qualification types that students can obtain while completing a QCF course: Award (only 1–12 credits are needed); Certificate (13–36 credits) and Diploma (over 37 credits). Compared to NVQ courses, a QCF course is generally more flexible and easier to complete, enabling even those in full-time work to undertake this qualification, while at the same time allowing the unemployed to balance interviews with their studies. Similarly, students can enjoy the benefits of being able to use the same credits across different units.

In 2015, a new Regulated Qualifications Framework (RQF) was introduced, that covers all attainments at all levels. The RQF can be understood as a 'bookcase' (see Figure 2.1), using levels to indicate difficulty, complexity and size in order to demonstrate the different study and assessment times. The QCF has been completely discarded by 31 December 2017 (Ofqual, 2018). There are small differences in the level descriptors and terms used in the RQF and the QCF, to reduce misunderstandings present in the QCF (Ofqual, 2018). The difference between the two systems is said to be that the QCF is more prescriptive, while the RQF is considered more descriptive (Ofqual, 2018). There are three designations of QCF qualification based on credit size: Award, Certificate and Diploma, ranging from entry level to Level 8 (Blinko, 2011). Although these titles can be used under the RQF, they are defined by Total Qualification Time (TQT): the credit value is allocated by the awarding body but must be equal to a tenth of the TQT assigned to that qualification (Ofqual, 2018). In addition, the QCF is built up from units of learning and credit values according to the levels of difficulty; whereas, in the RQF, the learning hours, including assessment time, are built up towards the TQT. In other words, at same level, different qualifications could take a different

TQT, or different levels could have a similar TQT. It can be seen that the RQF tends to include a range of learning forms including individual study, with assessment being performed at the workplace as well as in taught courses (Benson, 2015). The RQF appears to be more flexible; however, it may also increase the difficulty in identifying so-called 'learning hours' in an informal setting.

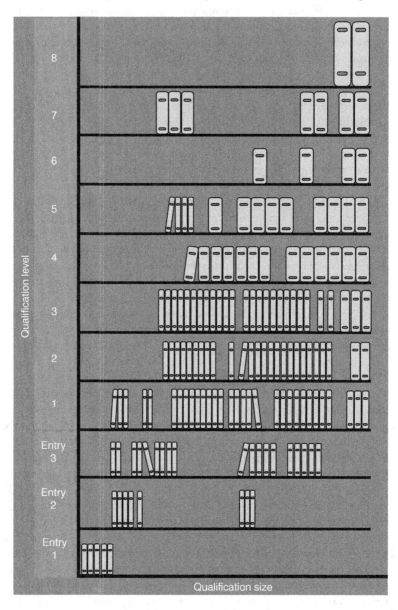

Figure 2.1 Regulated Qualifications Framework in UK.
Source: Ofqual.

To sum up, the UK qualification framework provides a relatively high level of flexibility for students. It is debatable whether such flexibility leads to 'fragmented skill sets' which trap individuals in low-skill sectors of the economy. Furthermore, the system is essentially an assessment rather than a learning or training programme. The UK does have a number of world-class apprenticeship schemes, particularly in the engineering sector. However, during the apprenticeship, it remains possible for students to complete an apprenticeship largely by having their existing skills accredited, with little new training involved.

Japanese VET system

Japan's reconstruction of its nation to become a great economic power in less than 40 years after its defeat in World War II has been a remarkable exception in modern economic history. Before the defeat in 1945, all of Japan's strength was directed towards gaining power through war. After the defeat, a high proportion of the industrial and commercial buildings together with the equipment they contained had been destroyed. As a result, the surviving Japanese people returning to their country from the war were left with chaos, starvation and unemployment. Even though Japan was left in ruins, its reconstruction from a fresh start is amazing. Japan's VET system is one of the key factors allowing it to achieve this 'economic miracle'.

During the first decade after World War II (1950s), the need for VET was widely accepted in Japan. Consequently, the Japanese government played a dominant role in the provision of vocational training, establishing national economic goals, setting up and overseeing a framework for VET. In the 1960s, the enactment of the Vocational Training Law of 1969 and its subsequent amendments laid down the fundamental principles of Japanese VET in terms of the roles to be played by various parties (i.e. government and enterprises). In this regard, the government began to scale back its involvement in the facilitation and supplementation of training programmes. Through the Ministry of Labour, the government assisted in running a National Institute of VET which focused on training instructors for industrial and public training centres as well as providing substantial subsidies to encourage small- and medium-sized companies to set up internal training programmes. It also oversaw a national system of trade testing which aimed at encouraging workers to attend additional training. The primary responsibility for providing VET thus rested with the enterprises. In the 1980s, the importance of such enterprise-oriented vocational training was further reinforced by the enactment of the Human Resource Development Promotion Act in 1985, which promoted industry-oriented vocational training by authorising on-the-job training and introducing flexible criteria for training to reflect the different needs of individual enterprises. Thus, government and individual enterprises in Japan shared different responsibilities in the provision of VET.

To be specific, in the Japanese public school system, vocational education courses are provided to students who enter upper secondary schools, resulting in three combinations of courses: general and vocational (4.7%), general only

(72.3%) and vocational only (23%) (NCEE, 2018). The general courses target students who are academic and aspire to university study, while the vocational courses are intended for the students who seek employment after graduation. The duration of the courses differs between full-time, part-time and correspondence. The full-time courses normally last three years and are subject to a competitive entrance examination. The part-time courses last four years and can be delivered as evening courses, catering for the majority of part-time students, or day courses. Furthermore, the curriculum covers a broad occupational range, including areas such as industry, agriculture, commerce, home economics and information technology.

In addition to the upper secondary schools, technical colleges also provide vocational education. These colleges were introduced in 1962, based on the British vocational education model and offer young school leavers a five-year programme of training as technicians in areas such as mechanical, electronic engineering, industrial chemistry and draughtsmanship (Cantor, 1985). In addition to formal and public schools, other providers of VET include miscellaneous schools and special training schools. Most of these schools are privately owned and provide courses which are approved by the Ministry of Education. They offer practical education and training in areas such as dressmaking and bookkeeping, which can be considered a supplement to courses offered by public VET schools.

Vocational schools in Japan account for one-quarter of the country's VET education capacity, the rest being provided by individual enterprises who show strong commitment to providing VET, especially vocational training to their employees (NCEE, 2018). Traditionally, these enterprises hire employees directly from universities or upper secondary schools with little or no previous industrial experience or training. In Japan, employment is regarded by both employers and employees as a lifetime contract and Japanese companies normally promote only from within their own ranks. Japanese companies thus feel it is desirable and obligatory to provide an internal programme for continuous education and training at all levels in the organisation. Based on this underlying philosophy, initial trainings are provided to newly recruited employees, updating trainings are for current employees, upgrading trainings are for the national trade test, and occupational capacity redevelopment trainings are provided to redundant employees to be job-ready. These training activities are exemplified by large corporations such as Toyota, Panasonic and Hitachi. For instance, Toyota has established the Toyota Institute, an internal organisation for training its executives and middle management, and overseas affiliates in the Toyota Way. The institute offers global leadership programmes to 180 future global leaders worldwide every year to develop their executive human resources capacity and leadership from a global perspective. Management development programmes are also provided to 300 middle managers worldwide every year to ensure that they can systematically understand and implement the Toyota Way.

Although the cooperative effort between government and enterprises contributes to Japan's economic prosperity, its VET system has its limitations. Since the responsibility for VET has largely lain with the enterprises, vocational training is neglected in schools. Schools focus on general education rather than apprenticeships to bridge and smooth students' transition from school to the workplace. Enterprises, on the other hand, attempt to reduce personnel costs by increasing the number of non-regular employees (i.e. part-time workers, dispatched workers and contract workers). The non-regular employees do not benefit from the same training opportunities available to the regular employees; in other words, they miss the opportunity to accumulate job skills through in-house training offered by enterprises to their regular employees. Thus, the mismatch between employee skills and demand from enterprises.

Chinese VET system and reform

Since the founding of the People's Republic of China in 1949, China has developed into the second largest economy in the world, with the world's largest population but with limited resources. The development of China's education system presents a significant problem, particularly considering the huge population base. In the past few years, China's education system has been undergoing transformation in order to cope with the requirements of rapid economic development and the growing demand for a more highly skilled workforce.

The most rapid development of the education system has taken place since the 1980s. From 1986, nine years of schooling became compulsory by law, including six years of primary and three years of lower secondary. By 2004, primary schooling became a universal system and 98.7% of students were enrolled in lower secondary school (Ministry of Education of People's Republic of China, 2017). In 2016, 87.5% of students were enrolled in upper secondary schools, which are attended after the end of the nine-year compulsory education. Access to upper secondary schools is by examination and upper secondary schools are primarily academically oriented, aimed at university entrance. Unlike the increase noted in academic education, secondary vocational schools numbered 10,900 less in 2016 than in 2015. In the same year, the total number of secondary vocational students was 15,990,000, which was 577,000 less than that in 2015. Out of the total number of students who studied at upper secondary schools in 2016, vocational students accounted for 42.5%, lower by 0.5% compared to 2015 (Ministry of Education of People's Republic of China, 2017).

Although vocational education has grown along with general education, it has appeared to lag behind. Secondary vocational schools were introduced in the 1960s, but this policy was reversed in the 1970s because of the view that these structures promoted social differentiation. During the 1980s, the emphasis on vocational education was renewed, and since the 1980s, VET has expanded substantially.

In China, formal VET is provided through separate secondary schools and tertiary institutions rather than through vocational programmes within a general secondary school or community-type college. Lower secondary vocational schools are rare and primarily located in rural areas where the economy is less developed. Graduates of lower secondary vocational schools become farmers and lower-skilled workers. Students in lower secondary vocational schools can take the examination to move on to upper secondary schools, but most students who enter upper secondary school come from the junior secondary general school. At the upper secondary level, there are four types of vocational schools: the first consists of general-vocational schools which are funded and managed by the Ministry of Education. They provide three-year certificate courses. The second type consists of specialised vocational schools, some of which are funded by the Ministry of Education and others are funded by industry and large state-owned enterprises (SOEs). These schools also provide a certificate at the end of the three-year study period. The third type of vocational school is represented by vocational high schools that have been transformed recently from general senior high schools. After graduation, students either enter the labour market directly or go on to tertiary vocational colleges. The fourth type consists of skilled worker schools which provide three-year certificate courses for state occupational licences. Figure 2.2 demonstrates the VET system in China.

Tertiary vocational education started in the 1980s but developed mainly from the mid-1990s onwards, recruiting mainly graduates from general high schools and secondary vocational schools. There are four types of VET institutions at the tertiary level: vocational-technical colleges or polytechnic colleges that provide two- or three-year diploma courses; specialised junior colleges that provide two- or three-year diploma courses, mainly for capacity building rather than technical training; technician colleges that provide two- or three-year certificate courses for state technician licences; and adult higher educational institutions that provide full-time and part-time certificate courses for knowledge enrichment and self-improvement. Vocational students can access tertiary VET institutions or universities by sitting the specialised college entrance examination held by these tertiary VET institutions or universities.

Beyond the diploma programmes in the formal VET education system, a range of non-diploma programmes are provided by secondary and tertiary vocational schools and colleges as well as other providers. Since 1978 industry has played and continues to play an important role in China's VET although it is hard to find data on the extent of this training. SOEs, for example, ran their own schools and provided training to their workers in a way that created an automatic connection between training and jobs. This sector of VET is now being phased out and responsibility shifted to the Ministry of Education as the restructure of SOEs as well as the role of SOEs in the economy is changing. The army provides a great deal of technical training, as do some industry associations. In some fields such as Chinese opera, medicine and martial arts, traditional apprenticeships continue the tradition of passing the craft on from one generation to the next. In recent years, there has been a significant growth of privately owned commercial VET providers.

The administrative structure of VET is complex; it is divided primarily between the Ministry of Education, which focuses on occupational and technical

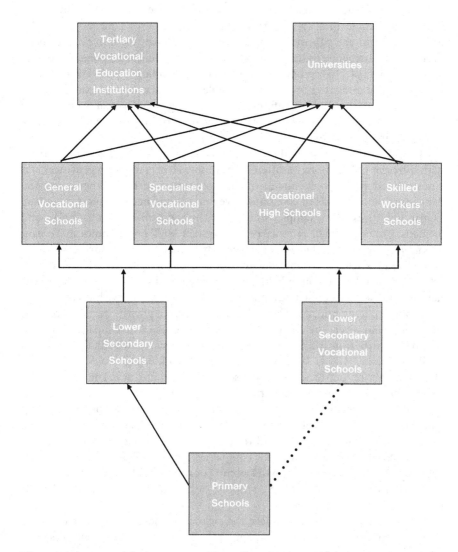

Figure 2.2 Structure of primary, secondary and tertiary vocational schools in China.

education, and the Ministry of Human Resources and Social Security, which focuses on skills training. However, there are other government entities involved in VET, such as the health department at provincial level and municipal level. Within the Ministry of Education, responsibility for education is divided between three main departments; namely, the Department of Fundamental Education (for pre-school and the nine years of compulsory education), the Department of Vocational and Adult Education (secondary VET and tertiary VET), and the

Department of Higher Education (universities). The Central Institute for Vocational and Technical Education, attached to the Ministry of Education, provides policy advice to the Ministry. The Ministry of Human Resources and Social Security Department of Occupational Capacity Building is responsible for the administration of VET programmes in technician colleges and skilled worker schools. These ministries are also responsible for developing occupational skills standards, assessing skills qualifications and issuing occupational licences; they also partner with vocational schools and set up job centres to run short-term skills training programmes around the country.

China does not have a single VET model as such since it is a large country with different jurisdictions in different locations. Hence, different provinces and cities may adopt different models of their own or learn from other countries, depending on their level of economic development and need for promoting particular industries. For example, some German companies, such as BMW and Siemens, provide a small number of dual system VET programmes in Yu'nan, Shandong, Hunan and Fujian provinces, where many manufacturing suppliers and related service companies operate. Colleges in the UK have partnered with schools in Shandong through British-style apprenticeships for similar reasons, as have Australian colleges in developing joint projects together with vocational institutions in Chongqing, and Canadian colleges working with vocational schools in Beijing. However, the foreign VET models adopted in China are not the original models from these countries, but have been modified. For example, unlike Germany, China lacks a statutory framework which would ensure the close cooperation between vocational schools and companies. The cooperation arrangements in China are mostly voluntary. Some German companies offer their company-specific (e.g. BMW) classes in a few vocational schools, enabling students to be trained with company-specific knowledge while they learn the fundamental vocational skills. Full-time students in vocational schools are offered practical training in different companies for one semester before graduation. However, unlike the German system, vocational students in China receive graduation certificates from their schools, rather than the standardised skills certificate from the industry.

In comparison with other models, the current Chinese way places a relatively heavy weight on school-based teaching while the hands-on experience is significantly less than in other countries, for instance, the dual system in Germany or modern apprenticeship in the UK. In addition, the status of VET in China is lower than that of academic education at university. This perception leads to low self-esteem, low motivation and low career satisfaction among vocational students as well as vocational teachers – something which is not common in other countries. Other issues faced by the Chinese VET system include a narrow VET curriculum, weak connections to industry, lower funding than academic education, few pathways between vocational education and academic education, and vocational teachers' lack of industry background. These issues will be elaborated in the following chapters with the presentation of our interview results.

Concluding remarks

In the past four decades, China has experienced a transformation from a rural and command economy into a global economic superpower. Human capital is one of the fundamental sources of its economic growth. To maintain and develop its human capital, the country requires investment and efforts from different parties. At individual level, these include individual efforts to obtain an education and training as well as professional development. At firm level, these include human resources development policies and practices such as training and development, aimed at increasing the aggregate firm-level human capital. At school level, an adequately designed curriculum and partnerships with enterprises are required to smooth students' school-work transition. At government level, the formation and implementation of adequate policies are required, as well as funding to education, especially VET institutions.

In comparison with other leading economies, China's VET system is still at the early stages, with a number of ongoing experimentations. However, none of the established international models, such as the German dual system and modern apprenticeships in the UK, can be adopted entirely. These models need to be modified and adapted to the reality in China by taking contextual and institutional factors (e.g. culture, policy and society) into consideration. In the next chapter, our review will trace back to the first vocational school established in China to illustrate the development of China's VET and the policies associated with its development. The review and analysis will provide logical understandings of the intertwined elements being adopted in China's current VET system and practices.

References

Aragon, I.B. and Valle, R.S., 2013. Does training managers pay off? *The International Journal of Human Resource Management*, 24(8), pp. 1671–1684.

Barney, J. B. and Wright, P. M., 1998. On becoming a strategic partner: The role of human resources in gaining competitive advantage. *Human Resource Management*: Published in Cooperation with the School of Business Administration, The University of Michigan and in alliance with the Society of Human Resources Management, 37(1), pp. 31–46.

Becker, G. M., DeGroot, M. H. and Marschak, J., 1964. Measuring utility by a single-response sequential method. *Behavioral Science*, 9(3), pp. 226–232.

Billett, S., 2015. *Integrating practice-based experiences into higher education*. Dordrecht: Springer Netherlands.

Birdi, K., Clegg, C., Patterson, M., Robinson, A., Stride, C. B., Wall, T. D. and Wood, S. J., 2008. The impact of human resource and operational management practices on company productivity: A longitudinal study. *Personnel Psychology*, 61(3), pp. 467–501.

Blinko, L., 2011. New employer-led vocational qualifications now available. *British Journal of Healthcare Assistants*, 5(3), pp. 141–143.

Cantor, L., 1985. Vocational education and training: The Japanese approach. *Comparative Education*, 21(1), pp. 67–76.

Coff, R. W., 2002. Human capital, shared expertise, and the likelihood of impasse in corporate acquisitions. *Journal of Management, 28*(1), pp. 107–128.

Colley, H., Hodkinson, P. and Malcolm, J., 2002. *Non-formal learning: Mapping the conceptual terrain, a consultation report.* Leeds: University of Leeds Lifelong Learning Institute.

Conger, R. D., Conger, K. J. and Martin, M. J., 2010. Socioeconomic status, family processes, and individual development. *Journal of Marriage and Family, 72*(3), pp. 685–704.

Eichhorst, W., Rodriguez-Planas, N., Schmidl, R. and Zimmermann, K. F., 2015. A road map to vocational education and training in industrialized countries. *ILR Review, 68*(2), pp. 314–337.

Eraut, M., 2004. Informal learning in the workplace. *Studies in Continuing Education, 26*(2), pp. 247–273.

Federal Ministry of Education and Research, 2018. [online] https://www.bmbf.de/en/index.html Available at https://www.bmbf.de/en/the-german-vocational-training-system-2129.html [accessed on 30 December 2018]

Federal Statistical Office of Germany, 2016. [online] https://www.destatis.de/EN/Homepage.html Available at: https://www.destatis.de/EN/FactsFigures/_CrossSection/Refugees/Refugees.html [accessed on 30 December 2018]

Frey, B. S. and Jegen, R., 2001. Motivation crowding theory. *Journal of Economic Surveys, 15*(5), pp. 589–611.

Garavan, T. N., Carbery, R. and Rock, A., 2012. Mapping talent development: Definition, scope and architecture. *European Journal of Training and Development, 36*(1), pp. 5–24.

Gerrard, J., Albright, J., Clarke, D. J., Clarke, D. M., Farrell, L., Freebody, P. and Sullivan, P., 2013. Researching the creation of a national curriculum from systems to classrooms. *Australian Journal of Education, 57*(1), pp. 60–73.

Harbison, F. H. and Myers, C. A., 1964. *Education, manpower, and economic growth: Strategies of human resource development.* New York: Tata McGraw-Hill Education.

Higgins, M. C. and Kram, K. E., 2001. Reconceptualizing mentoring at work: A developmental network perspective. *Academy of Management Review, 26*(2), pp. 264–288.

Hirschi, A., 2010. The role of chance events in the school-to-work transition: The influence of demographic, personality and career development variables. *Journal of Vocational Behavior, 77*(1), pp. 39–49.

Jorgensen, P. C., 2013. *Software testing: A craftsman's approach.* Boca Raton: Auerbach Publications.

Karmel, T. and Nguyen, N., 2006. *The value of completing a vocational education and training qualification.* National Centre for Vocational Education Research Ltd. PO Box 8288, Stational Arcade, Adelaide, SA 5000, Australia.

Klein, H. J. and Weaver, N. A., 2000. The effectiveness of an organizational-level orientation training program in the socialization of new hires. *Personnel Psychology, 53*(1), pp. 47–66.

Knowles, M. S., Holton III, E. F. and Swanson, R. A., 2012. *The adult learner.* New York: Routledge.

Koen, J., Klehe, U. C., Van Vianen, A. E., Zikic, J. and Nauta, A., 2010. Job-search strategies and reemployment quality: The impact of career adaptability. *Journal of Vocational Behavior, 77*(1), pp. 126–139.

Kreitzer, M. J. and Klatt, M., 2017. Educational innovations to foster resilience in the health professions. *Medical Teacher, 39*(2), pp. 153–159.

Liu, X. and Batt, R., 2010. How supervisors influence performance: A multilevel study of coaching and group management in technology-mediated services. *Personnel Psychology*, 63(2), pp. 265–298.

Marsick, V. J. and Watkins, K. E., 2001. Informal and incidental learning. *New Directions for Adult and Continuing Education*, 2001(89), pp. 25–34.

Mathieu, J. E., Tannenbaum, S. I. and Salas, E., 1992. Influences of individual and situational characteristics on measures of training effectiveness. *Academy of Management Journal*, 35(4), pp. 828–847.

McIntosh, S., 2004. *The impact of vocational qualifications on the labour market outcomes of low-achieving school-leavers*. London: Centre for Economic Performance, London School of Economics and Political Science.

Ministry of Education of People's Republic of China, 2017. [online] http://www.moe.gov.cn/s78/A03/ Available at: http://www.moe.gov.cn/jyb_xwfb/xw_fbh/moe_2069/xwfbh_2017n/xwfb_20170928/mtbd/201709/t20170929_315705.html [accessed on 16 January 2019]

Müller-Jentsch, W., 2018. Seven decades of industrial relations in Germany: Stability and change through joint learning processes. *Employee Relations*, 40(4), pp. 634–653.

National Institute of Adult Continuing Education, 2013. [online] https://www.local.gov.uk Available at: https://www.local.gov.uk/sites/default/files/documents/skills-build-creating-hou-751.pdf [accessed on 30 December 2018]

NCEE, 2018. [online] http://ncee.org Available at: http://ncee.org/what-we-do/center-on-international-education-benchmarking/top-performing-countries/japan-overview/

Office for National Statistics, 2017. [online] https://www.ons.gov.uk Available at: https://www.ons.gov.uk/peoplepopulationandcommunity/populationandmigration/populationestimates/bulletins/annualmidyearpopulationestimates/mid2017 [accessed on 30 December 2018]

Ofqual, 2018. [online] https://www.gov.uk/government/organisations/ofqual Available at https://www.gov.uk/guidance/vat-on-education-and-vocational-training-notice-70130 [accessed on 20 December 2018]

Paul Dana, L., 2001. The education and training of entrepreneurs in Asia. *Education + Training*, 43(8/9), pp. 405–416.

QCDA, 2010. [online] https://webarchive.nationalarchives.gov.uk/ Available at: https://webarchive.nationalarchives.gov.uk/20110215111801/http://www.qcda.gov.uk/qualifications/qcf/581.aspx [accessed on 29 December 2018]

Raelin, J. A., 1997. A model of work-based learning. *Organization Science*, 8(6), pp. 563–578.

Report on Vocational Education and Training, 2018. [online] https://www.bmbf.de/en/index.html Available at: https://www.bmbf.de/pub/Berufsbildungsbericht_2018_englisch.pdf [accessed on 30 December 2018]

Rock, A. D. and Garavan, T. N., 2006. Reconceptualizing developmental relationships. *Human Resource Development Review*, 5(3), pp. 330–354.

Ruona, W. E. A., 1998. Systems theory as a foundation for HRD. In *Proceedings of the 1998 Academy of Human Resource Development Conference*. Baton Rouge, LA: Academy of Human Resource Development.

Ryan, P., 2001. The school-to-work transition: A cross-national perspective. *Journal of Economic Literature*, 39(1), pp. 34–92.

Ryan, P., Gospel, H. and Lewis, P., 2006. Educational and contractual attributes of the apprenticeship programmes of large employers in Britain. *Journal of Vocational Education and Training*, 58(3), pp. 359–383.

Schultz, T. W., 1960. Capital formation by education. *Journal of Political Economy,* 68(6), pp. 571–583.

Wang-Cowham, C., 2011. Developing talent with an integrated knowledge-sharing mechanism: An exploratory investigation from the Chinese human resource managers' perspective. *Human Resource Development International, 14*(4), pp. 391–407.

Wilson, E. O., 2012. *On human nature.* Cambridge: Harvard University Press.

Wilson, W. J., 2011. *When work disappears: The world of the new urban poor.* New York: Vintage.

3 The development of VET in China

The development of VET in China is crucial at a national level for the overall development of human capital as well as the nation's competitiveness. VET lies fundamentally at the interface of the process of national industrialisation and economic development, as well as the improvement of working life at an individual level. More specifically, VET is an important way of improving human capital in order to excel in manufacturing high value-added, high-quality and advanced technological products. VET offers an alternative career path to those who cannot or are unwilling to undertake an academic education but wish to develop vocational skills. A greater access to VET education reduces poverty and inequality, and secures a society's continuity and progress. A VET education assists individuals, especially the youth, to identify with and become competent in their occupations with relevant skills. Furthermore, such an education is beneficial in sustaining occupational capacities and employability throughout employees' working lives in an ongoing career path.

In order to understand the current situation in China's VET system, it is essential to study its evolution. China's VET system has developed over the past 150 years and is the outcome of choices, compromises and decisions made among policymakers, educators, students and their parents, and the wider community, reflecting specific historical, social, economic and cultural circumstances. Reviewing these elements ensures an in-depth understanding of the current status, paving the way for the future development of China's VET system. The following sections illustrate the historical development over different periods, including the pre-liberation period before 1949 and post-liberation period to the present.

Prior to the founding of the People's Republic of China (PRC)

The period 1862–1948 was a time of political turmoil in China. The country faced pressure from Western colonial powers to move towards openness, as well as the appeal of modernisation and industrialisation. Modern schools were built under the motto 'Chinese learning is for the sake of essence, Western learning is for the sake of utility' (Lary, 2007, pp. 15–16). With the downfall of the

Qing dynasty in 1911, the new Republican government as well as other regional governments, educators and business communities shared the aspiration and responsibility for establishing a modern education system in China. Their efforts continued through the years of the Republic until 1949.

In imperial China, Confucian culture exerted a strong influence. Confucius (551 BC–479 BC) and his followers dominated the content of teaching, the institutions of learning and determined the way the Chinese viewed education and vocational education. From an early age, children were instructed to learn the *Analects,* followed by the *Classic of Filial Piety*, expanding to more advanced Confucian classics. According to Confucius, education enabled an individual to become an 'exemplary person' (*jun zi*) by nurturing their innate goodness and thereby becoming responsible for maintaining the order of society. Building on this view, as well as on the Confucian concept of recognition based on merit, rather than on birthright, the imperial examination system was introduced to recruit officials, based on a sophisticated literati-bureaucrat system. The imperial examination was created and monitored by the imperial court, and used to select bureaucrats from the best candidates. Candidates were tested on a variety of topics, ranging from an expanded list of the Nine Classics and policy questions to the composition of essays on government policies, miscellaneous essays (e.g. poetic writing), law, history and philosophy. Students were admitted to a social elite through several extremely competitive examinations. Besides enjoying social privileges (e.g. exclusion from labour service and special tax deduction) and the income of the bureaucratic classes, the grey income of a bureaucrat was estimated to be 14 to 22 times higher than the official salary (Ni & Van, 2006). In other words, the foremost purpose for students pursuing an education was to succeed in the imperial examination, which led to extraordinarily high economic and social status. Therefore, public and private schools were dedicated to instructing students to memorise the *Four Books*, the *Five Classics* and to write elegant essays, known as 'eight-legged essays.'

With the excessive deference to and reliance on Confucianism in its education and examination system, Confucianism became highly entrenched in both government and intelligentsias, and constituted the foundation for Chinese cultural norms. This trend was brought to great heights by the Qing government administration, especially in the late Qing period. The Qing rulers originated from the North as a minority group and utilised Confucianism to secure their position of power in its adoption of the mainstream cultural norms in order to gain cultural legitimacy. The Qing administration showed rigid adherence to Confucian thinking and opposed all things from the West, such as technology and science. Its opposition to the West was partly due to the institutionalised prejudice against new things as well as the Confucianism underlying Chinese educational tradition. Qing leaders stressed that a nation's greatness rested on its virtues, not on achievements in technology.

With the defeat in the Anglo-Chinese Wars (1839–1842, 1856–1860) and internal dissatisfaction with the Qing government, the reformist movement emerged in the 1860s. Many Chinese intellectuals and politicians stressed that

China needed modern armaments and military industries; they wished to build a powerful and modern Chinese Navy. To realise this ambition, these intellectuals spurred the establishment of the first generation of China's new modern education system.

1862–1911

After China's defeat in the first and second Anglo-Chinese Wars, great concern was raised by the challenges posed by Western colonialism, resulting in fierce debate about how to respond to such challenges. Many intellectuals and politicians in China urged that it was necessary to adopt Western military technology and armaments. In 1844, Wei Yuan (1794–1856) wrote the *Illustrated Treatise on Maritime Kingdoms* and concluded that the Western powers had beset China because of their advanced military technology. He outlined a plan for maritime defence which included building ships, making weapons and learning the superior techniques of the West. Subsequently, the Self-Strengthening Movement was initiated which aimed to extricate China from reliance on the West. The first institution in China (*Tongwenguan*) to teach foreign languages was established in 1862, freeing Chinese diplomats from reliance on foreign interpreters. In 1866, the curriculum was extended to include the study of astronomy and mathematics. However, with some noble exceptions, the overall quality of students remained low.

Military leader Zuo Zongtang (1812–1885) claimed that warships purchased from the West were not suited to domestic military demands and that in-house shipbuilding should be a prerequisite for self-strengthening. Additionally, Zuo maintained that the increased number of Western cargo ships in coastal areas undermined the traditional industry and commerce in China. This view reinforced the importance of coastal defence and protection to local businesses. In 1866, Zuo submitted a plan to the Qing court, addressing Chinese naval issues. This submission resulted in the appointment of Shen Baozhen as the Director of Marine Affairs. Located at Fujian province's Mawei Seaport, the office of Marine Affairs reported to the central government directly. With the assistance of two French naval officers, Prosper Giquel and Paul d'Aiguebelle, who were on leave from the French Imperial Navy, 40 engineers and mechanics from Europe were recruited in order to create a modern naval force for China. The initiative involved setting up a Western-style naval dockyard, constructing a fleet of eleven 150 horsepower transports and five 80 horsepower gunboats, and establishing a naval yard school (known as the Fuzhou Naval Yard School) to train Chinese youths in navigation and marine engineering (Pong, 1987). The Fuzhou Naval Yard School was the first specialised and vocational school established during the Self-Strengthening Movement. The school cultivated a great number of high-quality graduates who were the first batch of talents for the Modern Chinese Navy.

The school was initially divided into two colleges. The 'front college' majored in shipbuilding. The subjects consisted of three components: language (French and English), specialised foundation subjects (e.g. calculus, geometry, physics, drafting and mechanical engineering), and core professional subjects (e.g. principles of steam engines, hull design and hull manufacturing). Textbooks were imported from France and courses were delivered in French. Students spent half of the day in the classroom focusing on academic knowledge and the other half in the factory or dockyard for the professional subjects as well as hands-on practice. The courses in the 'rear college' focused on navigation and marine engineering. The 'rear college' consisted of two majors, namely, ship steering and maritime management. All classes were delivered in English. Students who majored in ship steering needed to learn geometry, spherical geometry and algebra as common professional subjects, and meteorology, astronomy, theory of navigation and geography as core professional subjects. Students who majored in maritime management needed to learn the same common professional subjects, while their core professional subjects included engine drawing, structure and installation of steam engines, and knowledge of the instrument board.

The importance of language (i.e. English and French) and mathematics was well addressed in the school's curriculum framework. With such skill sets, students were able to understand the principles of shipbuilding and to draft designs in accordance with original editions of textbooks. Without the need for translation, students were able to access cutting-edge knowledge more quickly. In addition to being exposed to Western-style courses, students were required to read the *Classic of Filial Piety* and the *Sacred Edict* in order to foster sensibility and rationalism.

The duration of programmes in both the 'front' and 'rear' colleges was five years. After three years' school and factory learning, students who graduated from the front colleges were sent to shipyards for internships for another two years, providing them with opportunities to apply the theory and skills learned at school. Similarly, graduates from the rear colleges worked as cadets on school ships for two years.

Once graduated, students having achieved outstanding performance were selected for further study in Europe. For example, in 1877, six outstanding graduates including Yan Fu, Sa Zhenbing, Liu Buchan, Lin Yongsheng, Fang Boqian and Ye Zugui were sent to study at the Royal Naval College, London. Yan Fu (1854–1921) returned to Fuzhou Naval Yard School as a teacher and later transferred to Tianjin Naval College as Head and ended his career as the distinguished President of Peking University. Sa Zhenbing (1859–1952) was appointed Admiral-in-Chief of the Beiyang, Nanyang and Guangdong Fleets and then served as acting Prime Minister under the Beiyang Government. Liu Buchan (1852–1895) served as commander of Beiyang Fleet. Liu Yongsheng (1853–1894) served as the captain of the protected cruiser *Jingyuan*. Fang Boqian (1853–1894) served as the captain of the protected cruiser *Jiyuan* and Ye Zugui (1852–1905) served as the captain of the *Zhiyuan*.

Following the establishment of the 'front college' and 'rear college' in 1866, Fuzhou Naval Yard School founded a college for apprentices (*yipu*) in 1868, recruiting promising students with physical strength. These students worked in dockyards under the instruction of their mentors during the day and studied in the evening. In comparison to the students in the 'front college' and 'rear college', academic requirements for students in this college for apprentices were lower. Students were only required to learn the courses at the basic or intermediate level and become skilled workers after graduation. The college was similar to the current secondary vocational school.

Fuzhou Naval Yard School can be considered to be the first vocational institution in China. The school reflected the philosophy underlying VET, combining school-based teaching and work-based practices (front and rear colleges), as well as providing on-the-job training (college for apprentices). A number of vocational institutions emerged from the success of the school, such as Tianjin Naval College which was founded in August 1881. Compared with Fuzhou Naval Yard School, the college's curriculum indicated significantly increased complexity and variety. Courses covered infantry drill and firearms, which were not included in the Fuzhou Naval Yard School. In addition, Shanghai Machinery College, Hubei Commerce College and Tianjin Telegraph College were founded to impart modern scientific knowledge and promote industrialisation as quickly as possible.

In general, the establishment of Fuzhou Naval Yard School and the subsequent vocational institutions is associated with the needs of China to develop a modern Navy and stimulate industrialisation. The school's model combined school-based teaching and workplace practices: the school-based teaching laid the foundation for understanding theory and built students' sense of humanity, while the workplace practice ensured that students grasped the practical skills needed most in the workplace. The way these courses provided students with opportunities to learn and practice the skills necessary in an authentic industry setting is very close to the current characteristics of well-established VET models. The curriculum adopted for the courses required students to learn a foreign language, science and Chinese traditional classics; it enhanced students' adaptability to future changes and capacity to gain additional skills and knowledge. Upon graduation, outstanding students could be sponsored by the government to further their studies abroad or be promoted as bureaucrats. Students were presented with a clear pathway for future development. Education and vocational education development was unfettered by the social and cultural baggage of Chinese traditions, and was not systematically organised.

1912–1948

As discussed above, imperial China and its Confucian thinking, coupled with one of the most sophisticated and rigid examinations, determined how the Chinese perceived education for over a thousand years. In 1905, the Imperial examination system was abolished. In 1911, the first civil revolution against feudalism terminated the domination of the Qing dynasty. The collapse of the Qing dynasty did not stop the efforts to reformation and modernisation of the education system. On the contrary, the Republican and Regional governments passed three

Education Acts legislated in 1912, 1922 and 1928. For the first time in Chinese history, attending lower primary school (Year 1 to Year 4) became compulsory and female students enjoyed equal education opportunities in primary schools.

The legislation marked a new era in the systematic development of education and VET in China. The concept of education gradually progressed to include its role in promoting social and industrial efficiency, and providing training and preparation for a specific vocation. In 1911, the first significant statement on the theory of vocational education was proposed by Lu Feikui (1886–1941), Editor-in-Chief of the *Journal of Education* (*Jiaoyu Zazhi*). In his seminal work *Preface to World Educational Conditions (Shijie Jiaoyu Zhuangkuang Xu)*, he maintained that vocational education was necessary to solve the problems of citizens' livelihood. His ideas gained significant support after publication. In 1913, Chen Duxiu (1879–1942) in *New Youth* (*Xin Qingnian*) also emphasised the need for VET as a primary part of China's education system.

At the same time, a group of professional educators including Huang Yanpei and Cai Yuanpai took the initiative to expand VET in China. Cai Yuanpei (1868–1940) served as the first Minister of Education in the Republican government in 1912. Cai held the view that education should be an effective way towards social progress and should strive for modernised education in China based on democracy and science. Huang Yanpei (1978–1965) had travelled to Britain to observe its VET system. In 1917, with support from industries, he founded the National Association of Vocational Education of China in Shanghai. This was the first organisation in China whose mission was to study, provide and advocate for VET. The association helped students acquire knowledge and skills in agriculture, industry and commerce, and signified a new stage in the development of VET. In the same year, the first journal on VET, *Education and Vocation* (*jiaoyu yu zhiye*), was published, advocating that the aim of VET was to prepare the youth to make a living, to prepare individuals to serve society and to improve production in China and around the world. Based on this aspiration, the Chinese Vocational School was founded in 1918. The school's purpose was to enable students to acquire practical knowledge, become familiar with required skills, assimilate moral principles and improve productivity.

During this period, the Chinese business community also started to participate in VET. Some Chinese firms began donating money to vocational schools and established scholarship funds. For example, Chen Jiageng (1874–1961) was a businessman, educator and philanthropist who set up funds in Southeast Asia and contributed to the establishment of several schools, including primary schools, secondary schools, vocational schools and universities (present-day Jimei University and Xiamen University). Chen was actively involved and invested in the vocational schools. These vocational schools ranged from agriculture, navigation, marine production and commerce, as well as teacher training schools.

In addition to the establishment of vocational schools, a new focus of VET emerged during this period aimed at assisting graduates in finding jobs. In 1920, a vocational recommendation bureau was founded in order to provide relevant positions to suitable graduates with potential employers through official recommendations (Huang, 1931). This development can be considered as the embryonic form of job allocation and career counselling.

Although the National Association of Vocational Education and vocational schools received support and encouragement from business, educators and political leaders, VET did not expand as expected. Besides financial hardship, another major difficulty identified was the fact that vocational schools regarded their primary function to be job training, while the majority of their students were determined to go on to higher education and had no intention of going out to find work after graduation. The vocational schools wanted to teach practical subjects, but the students wanted an increase in the number of general subjects as preparation for university study. Gradually, the vocational schools were changed into general schools or became neither general nor truly vocational (Zou, 1925).

From 1912 to 1948, the expansion of the modern education system including a VET system continued despite a number of wars and related interruptions, such as the Japanese invasion and the subsequent civil war. Government, business communities and educators undertook repeated and joint initiatives to progress the VET system. The vocational school founded by Huang formed the foundation of the present VET system and helped to establish the theories underlying the sector in China today (e.g. vocational schools should be designed to fulfil social needs and provide career guidance and counselling to graduates). However, the political turmoil, ongoing wars, slow economic progress and industrial development, as well as preference for academic excellence, hampered the development of VET during this period.

After the establishment of the People's Republic of China (PRC) in 1949

Educational development in China was confined to the political system and ideology, and was hindered by socio-economic development. On 1 October 1949, the People's Republic of China was established. It marked the victorious culmination of years of revolutionary struggle led by the Chinese Communist Party against domestic feudalism and foreign imperialism. The early 1950s and 1960s marked the beginning of China's rapid industrialisation. The country focused on building the national economy by following the Soviet model. A strong central government channelled scarce resources into heavy industry. The Chinese government held tight control over education policy and acknowledged that the economic modernisation campaign needed a better-educated workforce and to break the elite classes' monopoly on education. During these decades, public order improved and the march to socialism seemed to progress at a steady pace.

In the 1970s, the leaning towards the Centralized Planning Model progressed further. During the Cultural Revolution, the administration of educational institutions was paralysed and classes were suspended. The closing down of schools in this period left a gap that characterised a low quality of students.

After a variety of radical actions taken by the Chinese government in the 1980s, the reform focus shifted to urban areas. China's economic systems were redirected to the market and the opening of the economy to the outside world. This market-oriented economic system brought great changes to the economy and created an environment in which skills and knowledge, as well as the ability to learn, had a large payoff, but it also increased education inequalities.

In the 1990s, China's economy started to embrace market mechanisms allowing certain people and areas to become rich first. With marketisation, workers' incomes were closely associated with their abilities and skills, which further justified the importance of education or vocational education in China.

With the beginning of the 21st century, numerous educational policies have been developed by the central government as well as the relevant ministries and departments. These policies have been centred on four national themes in China, namely the educational equality of every citizen, individual and social productivity, efficiency as a national priority based on practicality, and rejuvenation of the nation in the world.

1949–1965

This period witnessed the rapid expansion of VET schools to meet the needs of economic expansion. This expansion was evidenced by the formation of three major types of VET schools. The first type was represented by ordinary secondary teacher training schools. These schools were administrated by educational bureaucracies and focused on providing training to students who wanted to become primary school and kindergarten teachers. The setup of these schools was strictly planned as only two types of schools (one for primary school teachers and the other for kindergarten teachers) were allowed in each city. In addition, the number of students who could be admitted was strictly planned and controlled. Since graduates could be assigned as teachers immediately after graduation with 'cadre' status, the process was highly selective and popular among students at the time. The second type of VET school took the form of secondary technical schools, aimed at training middle-level cadres and managers. These schools were under the direct jurisdiction of ministries, departments or industries other than educational bureaucracies. Attending secondary technical schools was also popular among students because graduates were given 'cadre' status upon graduation, a prestigious and well-paid position at the time. The third type of VET school was aimed at producing skilled workers and was run by the Department of Labour. Unlike the previous two types of schools, graduates of this school could not obtain 'cadre' status after graduation. Since these schools were mainly for skilled workers, they were usually located within factories. Given the difference of training orientations, the first two types of schools adopted a curriculum structure identical to that of the Soviet Union, consisting of foundation courses such as political studies, mathematics, Russian in the earlier years and English in later years, specialised foundation courses (i.e. engineering drawing), and other core courses (i.e. product design). Skilled workers' schools emphasised skills training for a particular factory and graduates were sent to work in the factory in which these schools were located.

In 1951, at the first National Secondary Education Meeting, it was pointed out that the disproportion between general education and vocational education should be reformed. In 1953, the State Council instituted the *Guiding Principles for Developing Secondary Vocational Schools* with the purpose of rectifying and consolidating the system, developing it with a focus on improving quality and ensuring steady development and growth. Based on these principles, measures were taken to improve secondary vocational schools in China. In 1954, the State Council issued the *Decision on Improving Secondary Vocational Schools* and in the same year approved the *Regulation on Secondary Vocational Schools* issued by the Ministry of Education to reform and develop secondary vocational schools (China Vocational Education Yearbook, 2018).

In the early 1960s, skilled workers were greatly needed across all sectors in China due to the economic recovery after the three years of famine (i.e. 1959–1961). Consequently, the development of secondary vocational schools, especially agricultural schools, was accelerated. During this decade, China's VET initially experienced fast development with several vocational schools being established and a large number of students being enrolled. However, since the increase was too fast, the quality of education became problematic. In order to enhance the quality, the Ministry of Education decided to adjust the scale of VET in 1961 and in 1963, the Government issued the *Discussion on Drafts of the Work of Full-time Primary and Secondary Schools and Several Directions*, stipulating that the policy of developing both general education and VET should be carried forward (China Vocational Education Yearbook, 2018). Thus, the position of VET was resumed and put on the path of steady development once again.

1966–1976

During the ten-year Cultural Revolution, the development of education and VET was dramatically slowed. All schools, both general and vocational, were closed from 1966 to the end of 1968 when Mao Zedong (1893–1976) announced the reopening of schools. The majority of students were to be trained in the old schools and colleges were to integrate themselves with workers and peasants. Students were to be re-educated by these workers and peasants under the guidance of the correct political line, and were expected to thoroughly change their old ideology. Workers and peasants would welcome those who had changed and reformed themselves. Students born between 1947 and 1952 who attended lower and upper secondary schools in 1966 were presumed to have graduated and were required to work in rural areas or factories. Approximately 16,000,000 students were sent to rural areas from 1968 to 1976, accounting for 10% of the urban population at that time. Some students were enthusiastic to work in remote rural areas, but most were forced to leave their families. During their re-education, formal education was sparse, and training was utilitarian, teaching skills such as how to make steel or how to grow rice. The aim was to train 'barefoot' experts. By engaging students in physical production either on the farmlands or factories, peasants and workers reminded the students to reform themselves as 'petty bourgeoisie' and to become new proletarians as the peasants and workers themselves. Students became self-supporting and partially relieved the financial burden on government to support a potentially large number of unemployed. From the leadership perspective, by the time the students finished their re-education, they would be a trained skilled workforce with political loyalty towards the party and its leaders.

Overall, the Cultural Revolution reduced the classroom exposure of students to two or three years at every educational level. Learning from peasants and workers who had considerable practical experience was the key feature of the education system during these ten years. Students appeared to be well trained with practical skills similar to those imparted in VET. However, it is noticeable that the training was also closely associated with 'being red' (i.e. politically correct) and being 'reliable successors to revolution'.

1977–1985

In the late 1970s, following the end of the Cultural Revolution, entrance examinations for college were resumed and vocational schools were reopened. At that time, students who intended to enter secondary vocational schools, colleges and university were required to sit the same nationwide entry examination. This historic era of reform began with the policy of opening-up to the outside world and vitality in the development of VET. Since the Third Session of the Eleventh Central Committee of the Party in 1978, the Party and the government have encouraged the development of VET and have clarified the status and role of VET in the education system as well as in the country's development in the new era. At the national education summit in 1978, Deng Xiaoping (1904–1997) pointed out that education should meet the needs of the development of the national economy and that the ratio of different kinds of schools in the education system should be proportional, especially with regard to agricultural and vocational schools. Later, in 1979, the *Government Work Report* pointed out the urgent need to develop various secondary vocational schools within secondary education; this would help to solve the problem of unemployment among graduates (China Vocational Education Yearbook, 2018).

In 1980, the *Report on the Structural Reform of Secondary Education* was released by the Ministry of Education and the State Bureau of Labour and ratified by the State Council (Ministry of Education, 1981). The report stated that the structure of secondary education should be reformed and that reform should be consistent with the reform of the 'cadre system'. Reform was intended to lead to investment in and development of universities and vocational schools and raise the literacy level of workers. VET was to be developed to meet the needs of socialist modernisation and used as the main channel to recruit skilled workers. In 1981, Hu Yaobang, the former Party Secretary, pointed out that based on the skill needs in urban areas, the government should convert about one-third of lower and upper secondary schools into vocational schools (Ministry of Education, 1981). On the occasion of the Fifth National People's Congress in 1982, the Constitution of the People's Republic China was amended to universalise the nine-year compulsory education and develop secondary education, vocational education and tertiary education accordingly (Constitution of the People's Republic of China, 1982).

The year 1985 was a milestone for VET in China as the structural reform of secondary VET was enacted. This reform was driven by problems in the national economy in general and the labour market in particular. At the time, the Chinese labour market was experiencing a serious shortage of skilled workers as well as middle-level technicians as industrialisation speeded up. In terms of the schooling system, the nine-year compulsory education was implemented. The universality of the nine-year compulsory education resulted in the number of graduates from lower secondary schools exceeding the number of intakes into upper secondary schools. This development meant that not all lower secondary graduates could enter upper secondary schools and hence the provision of VET became essential. Entering upper secondary schools did not guarantee entrance to universities (Ministry of Education, 1985). To address these issues, the Party Central Committee announced the *Decision on Structural Reform of Education*, clearly stipulating that a VET system should be established (Ministry of Education, 1985). The system was to have a rational structure and intermediate stages from the lower to the upper level that corresponded to industrial sectors and connected with general secondary education. Given that VET was still very weak, effective measures were necessary to improve the situation and develop the sector. It was also clear that "a VET system that combines both elementary and higher levels, supported by different industries and with reasonable structures, should be established" (Ministry of Education, 1985). The *Decision on Structural Reform of Education* made clear the status and role of VET in modern society and promoted the development of VET.

1986–1995

In the late 1980s, the opportunities for entering universities remained limited. Graduates from upper secondary schools with middle and low rankings rarely succeed in university entrance examinations. The situation raised concerns about what these students would do after graduation or failure in university entrance examinations. At the same time, market-oriented elements continued changing the job market. The emergence of self-employment, the autonomy of staffing in many industrial and commercial units and the entrance of foreign investment contributed to new patterns in the job market. Concerns were raised about skills improvements in order to enhance productivity and the importance of skills-oriented education such as vocational education was highlighted. Led by educational bureaucracies, some middle- and low-ranking upper secondary schools were converted to vocational high schools. However, such a top-down conversion was not implemented as educational bureaucracies had expected. First, not all middle- and low-ranking upper secondary schools were capable of converting into vocational schools. More specifically, these generalist upper secondary schools taught academic subjects which required little equipment. In order to establish vocational schools, especially those offering industrial majors such as computer numerical controls and auto mechanics, equipment for students to practice was needed. Since most of these upper secondary schools could not afford to purchase such equipment, they could choose to teach on the basis of textbooks or set up majors which did not require significant investment in equipment, such as accounting, marketing and secretarial skills. However, such a compromise was problematic as the supply of students majoring in accounting would eventually exceed the need, resulting in increased unemployment rates. Second, in addition to the lack of equipment, sufficient qualified teaching staff was another difficulty faced by the upper secondary schools. Due to the lifelong tenure in Chinese schools, the existing teaching staff could not be fired; they had to be reassigned to teach new subjects. The common practice was to assign teachers who had taught Chinese literature to teaching marketing and those who had taught physics were assigned to teach engineering. Under certain extreme circumstances, the teachers who majored in music were required to teach auto mechanics. Third, to the vocational students and its families, their preference for general education instead of vocational education is evident given that people still think by using general education, the students can move back into academic-oriented education system later. Even with increased support from the government, not all vocational schools could recruit sufficient students and lacked sufficient government funding (a proportion of government funding was calculated based on the number of students). Teaching general education subjects was less costly and became a compromise decision made by the school management.

In addition to the conversion from general upper secondary schools to vocational schools, China started to introduce a VET system based on the German Dual system in 1989 because of the increased demand for skills in the job market. In 1991, the State Council formulated the *Decision on Energetically Developing VET*, which identified tasks and objectives for developing VET further in the context of Chinese economic and social development in the 1990s (Ministry of Education, 1991). VET was featured even more prominently with the release of the *Outline on Reform and Development of Education* in 1993. Drawn up by the Party Central Committee and the State Council, the Outline was aimed at mobilising the initiative of all departments, enterprises, institutions and other quarters of society to provide VET in multiple forms and at different levels (State Council, 1993). It required governments at various levels to attach great importance to VET, to create comprehensive plans instituting it and to develop VET energetically. The government introduced and implemented practices and policies such as increasing enrolment quotas for existing vocational schools and continuing converting general upper secondary schools into secondary vocational schools (State Council, 1993). There were a few notable features when implementing these initiatives. First, a decentralised approach was implemented where local governments, with help from industries, took responsibility for the development of vocational education under their jurisdiction. Specifically, local governments had to manage the development of VET schools of different types and industry areas. Second, policies in favour of the employment of vocational school graduates were adopted. This was achieved through qualification-based hiring and giving priority to hiring vocational graduates in relevant fields. Third, a school-enterprise partnership was established to improve the quality of vocational teaching staff. Vocational teachers were encouraged to pursue skills-based qualifications in addition to their teaching certificate. Vocational schools were also encouraged to invite experienced employees to hold lectures, sharing their insights with students and communicating with teachers (Ministry of Education, 1994).

Efforts to introduce Western VET models in China and to involve enterprise partners were evident. However, being at an early stage, further adjustments were required to make the Western models work better. German legislation, for instance, dictated that German companies were responsible for VET and tax exemptions were granted if these companies trained and recruited vocational students. Thus, German companies were given incentives to be part of the VET system. However, in China, the participation of companies was voluntary, largely depending on connections and the charisma of school headmasters. Through a partnership with vocational institutions, enterprises were obligated to assign their experienced employees to institutions as advisors and to deliver lectures. This arrangement was intended to provide vocational students with certain industrial insights. However, in reality, employees were forced to deliver lectures and were not paid well. From the schools' perspective, this arrangement was part of the partnership, but for companies, it was simply part of their employees' jobs. In addition, the strict control on vocational schools' funding further limited the monetary reward paid to the advisors.

The period 1986–1995 was a time of radical changes in the job market as a result of the market-oriented economy. The government made great efforts to reform and develop VET in order to meet these new changes and challenges. Although there were many deficiencies, such as a shortage of qualified teaching staff, a shortage of training equipment and a preference for general education, the progress made was impressive.

1996–1999

Following the structural reform of VET initiated in 1985, the *Vocational Education Law* was established and enacted in 1996 (Ministry of Education, 1996). For the first time in the history of China, the legal status of vocational education was recognised and qualification requirements for vocational school teachers as well as vocational schools were specified. A year later, in a report of the Fifteenth National Congress, President Jiang Zeming pointed out the need to implement the strategy of reinvigorating China through science, technology and education while keeping development sustainable, and to actively develop various forms of VET (Jiang, 1997). In 1999, building upon the 1996 *Vocational Education Law,* the Ministry of Education published the *Action Plan for Educational Revitalization Facing the 21st Century* (Ministry of Education, 1999). The plan called for the development of a more coherent VET system with improved connections among all levels of VET and between VET and general education. It also proposed establishing a specialised fund for the reform of the VET curriculum and the development of teaching material. Furthermore, it aimed to create 50 VET teacher and instructor training institutions, based on existing general and vocational higher education institutions (Ministry of Education, 1999). In terms of enrolments in VET institutions, the Action Plan stated that the current enrolment ratio between general and VET at the upper secondary level should be maintained (about 6:4). In the few areas that did not fall under the universal nine-year compulsory education, VET at lower secondary level was to be developed to fill the gap, whereas in areas with well-developed upper secondary education, the focus of VET development was to be on improving quality and efficiency of VET. With regard to the transition from school to work, the Action Plan required secondary VET schools to conduct a scientific study predicting labour market demands and to design flexible and diverse courses to cope with the changing industrial structure and demand (Ministry of Education, 1999). Finally, the Action Plan emphasised the importance of VET in rural areas. It proposed that farmers in rural areas should be trained within three to five years in order to acquire one to two practical skills in production to enable them to catch up with the overall social and economic development and improve their living standards. In the same year, a dual certificate system, namely Graduation Certification and National Vocational Qualification certificate, was introduced (Ministry of Education, 1999). VET was thus made more appealing to students and students' employability was increased.

Since the founding of the People's Republic of China at the end of the 20th century, China's education, both general and vocational, developed vigorously with many upheavals. It was well recognised that China's education system should adapt to the socialist market economy in which different types of education were integrated with each other, and that vocational education and senior secondary education (both general and vocational) needed to be actively developed. During this period, China's VET opened up to the world with the introduction of the international VET system. Great efforts were made to establish a curriculum framework in order to meet the needs of economic and social/cultural development.

2000–present

In 2002, the *Decision of the State Council on Energetically Promoting the Reform and Development of Vocational Education* (State Council, 2002) provided some guidance on the development of VET at all levels. Specifically, the Decision called for shaping vocational education to meet the needs of economic and social/cultural development. It was pointed out that VET should be related to the employment of the trainee and the education received should meet the needs of the market (State Council, 2002). The importance of developing VET for agriculture, rural areas and farming was also emphasised. In terms of educational funding, the Decision aimed to ensure that the government, rather than the private sector, was the primary supporter and provider for vocational education, while incorporating support from business, institutions and social groups (State Council, 2002). The Decision explicitly stated that no less than 15% of urban surtax for education expenditure should be allocated to vocational education. In areas with universal compulsory education, no less than 20% of urban surtax for education expenditure should be devoted to vocational education. At the same time, companies should allocate funds for employees' education and training at the rate of 1.5% of the total salary. For high-performing companies requiring advanced skills, the rate was to be 2.5%. Private financing of VET would be rewarded with favourable tax policies such as tax-deductible donations to VET (State Council, 2002). In 2005, three years after the 2002 Decision, the State Council issued another Decision regarding the development of VET (State Council, 2005). It provided updated guidance on the financing of VET and the regulation of the VET market at all education levels. The Decision reiterated the importance of a partnership between schools and companies, where the latter had the responsibility of providing training to VET students and teachers. Each industrial association was required to make predictions regarding the demand for vocational graduates in that specific industry, in order to provide guidance for the development of the VET curriculum and training schemes. The vocational qualification system was to be further improved and regulated, ensuring that workers with VET diplomas, vocational qualifications or training certificates were given priority in employment (State Council, 2005). The Decision called for the establishment of a VET financial aid system since a large share of VET participants were students from poor rural families or low-income urban families. Local governments were to develop financial aids, scholarships or student loans to provide tuition exemption, tuition reduction and living expenses subsidies to students as well as other disadvantaged groups. The Decision also encouraged public VET schools to be open to financing from the private sector as well as foreign enterprises. The development of private (*minban*) VET schools was also encouraged, as were improved relevant regulations on land use and financing of these private VET schools. Meanwhile, teachers at these private VET schools were to be treated the same as teachers in other public schools (State Council, 2005).

In 2010, the *Outline of China's National Plan for Medium and Long-term Education Reform and Development (2010–2020)* was approved at the State Council's executive meeting (State Council, 2010). The Outline was formulated to enhance overall skill levels, boost educational development in a scientific way and speed up socialist modernisation. Recommendations were made on increasing VET development since it was seen to be a channel for boosting economic growth, promote employment, improve people's livelihood and a key link in mitigating structural conflicts between skills supply and demand. The Outline emphasised that the government should play a leading role while industries should offer guidance and enterprises should participate in initiatives. A call was made for legislation to be enacted to advance and institutionalise cooperation between VET schools and enterprises (State Council, 2010). The National Vocational Student Skills Competition was launched by the Ministry of Education in 2013 to encourage VET development in China, with the participation of government departments and industries. The competition is a major national initiative aimed at vocational education with the profoundest influence, widest coverage and greatest student participation. Vocational schools compete with each other and emphasise the number of first prizes they win to prove the quality of their education. The schools cultivate a small number of students, using the best resources (e.g. best teachers and the most advanced equipment), and this group of students, in turn, are readily welcomed by companies. It is common to see HR personnel wait outside the competition venue, eager to offer positions to the students immediately after the competition results are released. However, it is debatable whether this competition pushes VET to extremes and potentially compromises other students' interests, deviating VET from its initial goals and resulting in VET becoming 'an elite education'.

The 40th anniversary of China's VET reform and opening-up was marked in 2018. The *Methods for Promoting Cooperation between Vocational Schools and Enterprises* was introduced and published by the Ministry of Education in association with five other ministries and departments. The Methods were an institutional framework for a vocational school-enterprise cooperation which established guiding principles, forms, promotional measures and supervision. An action plan was to be launched based on the Methods to establish over 1,000 pilot projects in 100 cities in ten provinces, and to further promote the integration of VET and business (Ministry of Education, 2018).

As part of the ongoing efforts to improve VET in China, a national pedagogical standards system for VET was created in 2018. This system provided catalogues of majors and programmes, vocational teaching and curriculum standards, standards for work placement and reports on skills demands. More specifically, the system included catalogues listing all the majors offered at secondary and higher vocational education institutions and related management methods, 230 vocational teaching standards for secondary vocational schools and 410 for vocational colleges, nine teaching syllabuses for required courses for secondary vocational schools and nine for vocational colleges, work placement standards for 136 majors, specifications for 19 categories of specialised instruments, skills demand forecasts for 60 industries and guidance for vocational education institutions on the introduction of degree programmes. The standards system served as an important basis for vocational schools to organise teaching and evaluation (Ministry of Education, 2018).

In addition to this initiative, the Ministry of Education issued the *Regulations on Strengthening Career Guidance in Secondary Vocational Schools* in 2018. The *Regulations* outline the principles for providing career guidance and career counselling. Subsequently, the *Circular on A Lifelong Professional Skills Training System* was released (State Council, 2018). The Circular signified an acknowledgement of students as an important part of a nation's human capital, with a focus on lifelong learning and continuing improvement of knowledge and skills.

In 2019, the State Council released the *National Vocational Education Reform Implementation Plan* (State Council, 2019). This plan clearly points out that VET in China needs to be reformed in order to complement science and technology development trends and market demands, as well as promote economic modernisation and higher quality employment. All sectors of society, especially enterprises, are encouraged to support vocational education, run vocational schools and offer high-quality VET programmes. Within five to ten years, operators of China's VET institutions, which are now mostly government-run, are expected to be diversified and to include more entities or personnel from non-government sectors. The plan details measures to improve national systems and policies relating to VET and lift the quality of both secondary and tertiary VET in China. It has introduced the pilot projects of the '1+X' certificate system. This system encourages vocational students to proactively pursue more than one skills qualification while studying in vocational institutions. Additionally, the government intends to establish national standards for VET and ensure standards regarding the teaching and curriculum framework are met, to nurture and pass down 'craftsmanship' skills nationwide. With regard to teaching in particular, from 2020 vocational institutions will not recruit fresh graduates to be vocational teachers. Applicants will need to obtain a professional qualification with a minimum of three year's work experience in order to be vocational teachers (State Council, 2019). Compared to the previously required half to one year's work experience, the three-year requirement represents a substantial increase. However, in comparison with the average five-year work experience required in developed countries, the three years do not appear to be long enough. The '1+X' system is a reflection of the government's determination to improve the quality of vocational teaching staff. The system has raised a question as to how graduates will find jobs. In the past five years, a number of normal vocational education universities have been founded. These universities aim to cultivate students who graduate with dual certificates (i.e. teacher's certificate and skill qualification) and become vocational teachers. Under the *National Vocational Education Reform Implementation Plan*, these graduates may not be qualified to be vocational teachers due to the lack of work experience. If graduates cannot achieve their plan of becoming vocational teachers, there is a need to assess whether educational resources are being wasted.

China's ambitions for the 21st century is to become an 'industrial superpower' by 2049, as outlined in the State Council's strategy paper. The action plan *Made in China 2025* lists specific measures and aims to achieve the first milestone in 2025. In order to become an advanced industrialised nation, the Chinese government needs to restructure the economic system, as well as the VET system. The structural reform of the VET system in China has run a long course, during which many plans were drawn up and a number of regulations established. However, this policy-driven structured reform has not taken place without problems. At a macro-management level, it has led to a mutual meeting among ministries (e.g. the Ministries of Education and the Ministry of Human Resources and Social Security) and departments under the leadership of the State Council. Given the complexities of China (e.g. geography, population and uneven economic development in different areas), a question emerges: how to implement plans and regulations to fulfil their intended goals. During the implementation, cooperation and coordination among different tiers of governments, various industries, schools, business and individuals are critical. For instance, the VET qualifications system in developed countries (i.e. Britain, Germany and Japan) is systematically developed and is under the clear jurisdiction of corresponding ministries. In China, the system is shared by different ministries, leading to arguments and conflicts. The Ministry of Education is in charge of issuing graduation certificates while the Ministry of Human Resources and Social Security oversees issues relating to skills (e.g. training, assessing and issuing qualifications); where the boundary lies remains arguable. Furthermore, continuous adjustment, correction, manifestation and improvement are essential and assure that China's VET is on the right track.

Since the establishment of the People's Republic of China, VET has developed through several stages. The focus has shifted from initially increasing the number of vocational schools to improving the quality of VET, to building China's own VET system and further integrating school-based learning and workplace training with a greater emphasis on quality rather than quantity, as Figure 3.1 demonstrates. The number of vocational schools decreased gradually, from 14,832 in 2007 to 10,671 in 2017. The major increase from 2002 to 2007 was caused by the exclusion of a vast number of skilled workers' schools before 2000. The exclusion was due to the fact that these schools were under the management of the Ministry of Human Resources and Social Security, not the Ministry of Education. Figure 3.2 shows the steady growth of students enrolled in vocational schools and vocational teachers, and the ratio between teachers and students which has gradually increased in recent years. This trend indicates that the overall quality of student learning and support from the VET system by teachers have gradually improved in recent years.

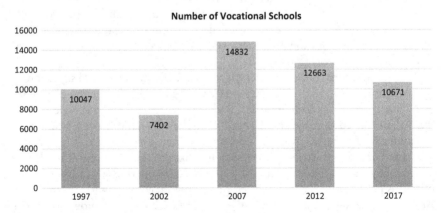

Figure 3.1 Number of vocational schools (1997–2017).
Data source: China's Ministry of Education, 2018.

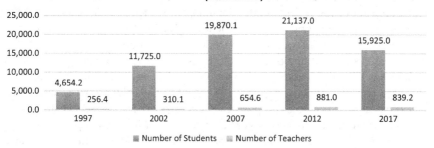

Figure 3.2 Number of students and teachers (1997–2017).
Data source: China's Ministry of Education, 2018.

Concluding remarks

In the late Qing dynasty, when China confronted the West, the gap between Chinese Confucian study and Western science-based education was exposed. Narrowly pursuing academic achievement resulted in delayed development in natural sciences and practical expertise, and China's backwardness in industrialisation. Under the slogan of 'being self-sufficient' and 'national development', education, especially VET, was initiated by the government to reform the old system and transform it into a modern system. The government provided students with opportunities to learn and obtain the necessary skills in an authentic industry setting and cultivated a number of high-quality graduates who made significant contributions to the movement of modernisation in China. The emergence of VET signified the first turning point in China's modernisation and industrialisation.

Following this trajectory, joint efforts were made by policymakers, educators and business leaders to push the development of modern VET in China. The focus shifted from 'save China' to 'rejuvenate China'. The traditional belief in academic excellence was challenged and the importance of practical skills emphasised. Education, especially the new VET system, prepared students to serve society and improve the production capability and competitiveness of China.

During the first decade after the establishment of the People's Republic of China, China's economic building and vocational schools followed the Soviet model. By focusing on achieving development in a scientific way, China has gradually developed a Chinese-style path of carrying out industrialisation since the 1980s. With deeper economic structural reforms, the change in China's economic growth model has accelerated. China has developed its own general and vocational models to cultivate a better-educated and higher-skilled workforce.

Although impressive progress has been made, the policies and regulations of China's VET are mostly government-driven with limited participation from industries, enterprises, schools and individuals. The responsibilities of each key stakeholder are not explicitly outlined and confirmed.

In addition, the status of VET in China is significantly lower than that of general education in the public mind. In comparison with general education, VET is insufficiently funded by the government and is a less favourable choice for students and their parents. Vocational education and vocational training are not well integrated. Graduates' employability and adaptability to future workplace changes remain low. The curriculum and textbooks are becoming obsolete and are not able to match the needs of the industry. Furthermore, vocational teachers lack proper vocational training and practical work experience. The school-enterprise partnerships have been formed voluntarily but are not fully developed. These are all issues faced by policymakers, educators, industry leaders, and students and their parents.

In the third wave of industrialisation, China has consolidated its industry chain. With the upcoming fourth wave of industrialisation, industries in China will change rapidly and will catch up with the trends of the digital economy and other new economic sectors. The fixed and centralised factories and massive labour forces may no longer exist. This change will shape the nature of work and will accelerate workforce reskilling, potentially leading to a totally different VET landscape. In order to cope with these changes and challenges, the government needs to plan well ahead of the current situation in which the VET system is designed and operated based on the third wave of industrialisation.

In the next chapter, we will demonstrate how individual vocational schools across different cities and provinces in China are organised, how they cooperate with government, industries and enterprises, and how they prepare students for a smooth transition from school to the workplace. We will also provide a basis for understanding the development trajectory of China's VET system at the grass-root operating level.

References

China Vocational Education Yearbook, 2018. Beijing: Economy and Management Publishing House.

Constitution of the People's Republic of China, 1982. [online] http://www.npc.gov.cn/npc/xinwen/node_2.htm Available at: http://www.npc.gov.cn/wxzl/wxzl/2000-12/06/content_4421.htm [accessed on 21 November 2018]

Huang, Y., 1931. Sanshiwu nian lai Zhongguo zhi zhiye jiaoyu [Chinese vocational education over the last thirty-five years], in Y. Zhang (ed.), Sanshiwu Nian Lai zhi Zhongguo Jiaoyu [*Chinese Education Over the Last Thirty-Five Years*]. Shanghai: Commercial Press, pp. 133–152.

Jiang, Zeming, 1997. Report to the Fifteenth National Congress http://cpc.people.com.cn/GB/64162/64168/64568/65445/4526285.html

Lary, D., 2007. *China's republic* (Vol. 2). Cambridge University Press.

Ministry of Education, 1981. *Education in China*. Beijing: People's Education Press.

Ministry of Education, 1985. [online] http://www.moe.edu.cn Available at: http://www.moe.edu.cn/publicfiles/business/htmlfiles/moe/moe_177/200407/2482.html. [accessed on 18 November 2018]

Ministry of Education, 1991. [online] http://www.moe.edu.cn Available at: http://www.moe.gov.cn/s78/A07/s8347/moe_732/tnull_8940.html [accessed on 21 November 2018]

Ministry of Education, 1994. [online] http://www.moe.edu.cn Available at http://old.moe.gov.cn/publicfiles/business/htmlfiles/moe/moe_177/200407/2483.html [accessed on 21 November 2018]

Ministry of Education, 1996. [online] http://www.moe.edu.cn Available at: http://www.moe.gov.cn/s78/A02/zfs__left/s5911/moe_619/tnull_1312.html [accessed on 21 November 2018]

Ministry of Education, 1999. [online] http://www.moe.edu.cn Available at: http://old.moe.gov.cn//publicfiles/business/htmlfiles/moe/moe_958/200506/xxgk_8944.html [accessed on 25 December 2018]

Ministry of Education, 2018. [online] http://www.moe.edu.cn Available at: http://www.moe.gov.cn/srcsite/A07/s7055/201802/t20180214_327467.html [accessed on 21 November 2018]

Ni, S. and Van, P. H., 2006. High corruption income in Ming and Qing China. *Journal of Development Economics, 81*(2), pp. 316–336.

State Council, 1993. [online] http://www.gov.cn/guowuyuan/ Available at: http://old.moe.gov.cn/publicfiles/business/htmlfiles/moe/moe_177/200407/2484.html [accessed on 25 December 2018]

State Council, 2002. [online] http://www.gov.cn/guowuyuan/ Available at: http://www.gov.cn/gongbao/content/2002/content_61755.htm [accessed on 21 November 2018]

State Council, 2005. [online] http://www.gov.cn/guowuyuan/ Available at: http://www.gov.cn/zwgk/2005-11/09/content_94296.htm [accessed on 25 December 2018]

State Council, 2010. [online] http://www.gov.cn/guowuyuan/ Available at: http://www.gov.cn/jrzg/2010-07/29/content_1667143.htm [accessed on 26 December 2018]

State Council, 2018. [online] http://www.gov.cn/index.htm Available at: http://www.gov.cn/zhengce/content/2018-05/08/content_5289157.htm [accessed on 25 February 2019]

State Council, 2019. [online] http://www.gov.cn/guowuyuan/ Available at: http://www.gov.cn/zhengce/content/2019-02/13/content_5365341.htm [accessed on 25 February 2019]

Zou, E. 1925. Canguan Jiangsu zhiye jiaoyu hou de ganchu yu jianyi [Impressions and suggestions after investigating the vocational education in Jiangsu]. *Jiaoyu Zazhi, 17*(7), pp. 26373–26375.

4 Case studies of VET in China

China has become a global production centre boasting of an impressive economic growth. It has shifted from an economy based heavily on low-cost and low-skilled manufacturing for export, to an economy based on high-quality and high value-added goods and services. Currently, the country is on the road to modernisation under the banner of innovative production and needs to invest in and upgrade the overall skill levels among the workforce. A critical shortage of skilled workers, qualified technicians and high-quality service providers exists across different areas and industries such as electronics, information technology, steel, equipment manufacturing, automobile, healthcare, finance and tourism. However, China's general education system has predominantly focused on academic studies which have led to a surplus of qualified academics without relevant practical experience. University graduates are not able to find jobs relevant to their degrees and must make significant compromises with respect to their job expectations.

VET focuses on acquiring practical skills which could provide relief from this mismatch. However, in China, VET needs to be reformed in order to meet such challenges. The vocational education institutions have been the main pillars of China's VET system. In contrast to the situation in Germany, the UK and Japan, Chinese vocational education institutions indicate insufficient coordination with enterprises, industry associations and trade unions. The VET curriculum framework is relatively narrow and out of date. Students remain passive recipients of education and training. Vocational teachers lack industry background and knowledge of cutting-edge technology. In order to enhance the quality of China's VET, great efforts have been made in many vocational schools and have met with success. We will demonstrate a number of such cases in the following sections.

During the past year, we visited vocational schools in China and selected eight representative cases. Most of these schools are located in the coastal regions which enjoy advanced economic development, while others are in rural rears and inland regions which represent different challenges and responses. In this chapter, we use these cases to illustrate how VET is organised in order to cope with the external and internal challenges to national and regional economic development, and describe the attempts made to improve the quality of education, learning from foreign experience, and engaging and cooperating with enterprises.

Background of case studies

China's VET is still at an early stage and is experiencing ongoing reform. Many pilot projects have been launched, such as the introduction of a Dual System similar to that of Germany, and lessons have been learnt from other countries such as the UK and Japan. Unlike the provision of general education which tends to be standardised across China, the provision of VET varies depending on local industrial structures, traditions, economic status and economic development needs. Given such variations, common factors contributing to the success of VET include the alignment with policy and overall national and local development directions, and suitability to the surrounding environment. Elements in this regard include: (1) schools' mission and vision organised in alignment with the direction of national and local economic development; (2) curriculum framework developed under the guidance of the mission and vision in order to be consistent with the needs of local economic and industrial development; (3) course content fulfilling the demands of the local labour market and requirements of enterprises; and (4) the training received suiting students and teachers' career development as well as personal preferences. In this section, we provide an overview of the case studies, identify several issues in China's current VET system and elaborate on how individual VET schools tackle each issue by coordinating all resources available.

Methodology and cases profiles

We have used case studies as the research method in this book. A case study is defined as "an empirical inquiry that investigates a contemporary phenomenon within its real-life context; when the boundaries between phenomenon and context are not clearly evident; and in which multiple sources of evidence are used" (Yin, 1984: 23). Case studies are widely recognised as a robust research method particularly when a holistic, in-depth investigation is required. This form of research has been applied in many areas and disciplines such as sociology, medicine, education and community-based problems. With regard to issues arising in education, the role of case study research is prominent (Gülseçen & Kubat, 2006). The case study method adopted in this book is exploratory and collective (Stake, 1995; Yin, 1994). We begin by exploring and investigating the VET phenomenon through a detailed analysis within a specific context. We then coordinate all data and information collected, which will allow for a generalisation of findings to a bigger population.

China has a vast territory and situations vary from region to region. We visited a number of secondary vocational schools and selected eight to present in this book as each school has its own unique characteristics (see Table 4.1). The eight schools selected were from Beijing, Shanghai, Jiangsu, Fujian, Guangdong, Shandong and Chongqing. The inclusion of these cities and provinces represents the northern (i.e. Beijing and Shandong), eastern (i.e. Shanghai), southern (i.e. Jiangsu, Fujian, and Guangdong) and inland (i.e. Chongqing) regions in

China. The selected schools cover major subjects, including computer numerical control, die and mould manufacturing, automobile, agriculture, catering and business administration. A skilled workforce in areas such as computer numerical control and die and mould manufacturing is urgently needed, both areas forming the foundation of China's innovative manufacturing development. In addition, the manufacturing sector in general and the automobile sector in particular are pillars of industry in China. Agriculture is also closely linked to people's daily lives. Service industries in general and the catering sector in particular are in expansion and are becoming a driving force of economic development. Business administration skills are also evolving and expanding along with participation in the global economy.

In order to protect the identity of the schools studied, the names were coded. No details that would substantially change the information collected were altered. An initial analysis process was undertaken by selecting and identifying concepts. Such concepts ranged from a general description such as classroom teaching, workplace practice and curriculum framework, to more detailed descriptions such as guiding principles, alignment between course content and skills needed, and collaboration between schools and enterprises. This was followed by a deeper analysis in order to interpret and summarise the conceptual constructs drawn from each case within the context of overall national and regional economic development in China.

VET plays a crucial role in the economic development of China; it is continuously subject to the forces driving change in society, industry and schools, and is shaped by the needs of the changing economy and local communities. In recognising the value and importance of VET, the relevant stakeholders, including the central and local governments, industries, enterprises, schools, teachers and students, need to ensure its relevance and responsiveness in the increasingly globalised and competitive economy.

VET schools located in different regions face different challenges in relation to regional economic development. By using different cases to illustrate the contextual environment and VET schools' responses, we are able to present an overall picture of the alignment between economic development and the role of VET schools to support this development. In particular, we have selected VET schools which are developing training programmes in the areas of design and manufacturing of dies and moulds, the automobile and agribusiness sectors in Shanghai, Fujian and Shandong respectively, located in sectors that have been the driving industries towards regional development.

The design and manufacturing of dies and moulds in Shanghai

The design and manufacturing of dies and moulds are a good example of the significant links in the entire production chain, given nearly all mass-produced discrete parts are formed using production processes that employ dies and moulds. The success of die and mould manufacturing is closely tied to the outlook of industries, especially high value-added industries. In China, die and mould

Table 4.1 Profiles of selected VET schools

School Codes	Location	Year of Establishment	No. of Students (in 2017)	No. of Full-Time Teachers (in 2017)	Characteristics
VET 01	Beijing	1980	326	150	• Strategic transition from vocational education to community training • Narrow scope of curriculum • New technology in teaching
VET 02	Shanghai	1959	3,207	206	• Strategic transition from chemistry to IT • Adopting marketing strategies for changes in labour market • Adopting intelligent and smart school management system
VET 03	Shanghai	1963	2,226	194	• Fostering of skilled workers needed most • Adopting delicacy management system • Watch repairing to rejuvenate local industry • Community service and care of disadvantaged groups
VET 04	Jiangsu	2005	8,173	582	• Modern Apprenticeship • Enterprise-school model with Chery Jaguar Land Rover
VET 05	Fujian	1978	5,136	287	• Dual System with BMW • Urban rail transit • Edited school textbook
VET 06	Guangdong	1964	5,840	257	• Toyota Class • Campus culture and cultivation of professionalism
VET 07	Shandong	1979	6,280	560	• VET for agriculture • Fostering of modern professional farmers • International cooperation with Southeast countries
VET 08	Chongqing	1909	5,000	230	• Education inequality in inland region • Modern female education • Strategic transition from general school to vocational school

Source: Interviews conducted in 2018 Alignment between VET and economic development.

manufacturing technology has been identified as one of the most important technologies since China's sixth Five-Year Plan (State Council, 1980). With 30 years of development, China has become an important die and mould manufacturing and consumption power in the world. Currently, China's die and mould manufacturing is entering a critical period aimed at improving precision and quality. Under such circumstances, offering training with a high-quality major subject in die and mould manufacturing technology is important to regional and national industrial development.

Shanghai is one of the four municipalities under the direct administration of the central government in China. Located on the Pacific Ocean and in the central section of the north-south coastline of China, Shanghai has served as one of the major trading ports and gateways to inland China since the mid-19th century. Since the economic reform started in the late 1970s, Shanghai has achieved rapid and sustained growth. Its manufacturing industry has long played a supporting and driving role in its economy. Although currently the ranking of its total manufacturing output has dropped, Shanghai has a strong industrial base and advantages in terms of manufacturing industry, such as production scale, industrial structure, labour productivity, comprehensive matching capacity, talent pool and resource allocation. Shanghai's well-developed iron and steel, automobile, and petrochemical industries remain competitive. The city has a full-range industrial chain in manufacturing, which is unique even amongst the world's major industrial cities; its industrial structure is balanced, with an appropriate heavy-to-light industry ratio and suitable shares between primary, secondary and tertiary industries (Yearbook of Shanghai, 2017).

Shanghai is also home to the VET03 school which has been one of the leading schools for many years. In 1998, the school merged with another secondary vocational school offering strong mechanical and electrical majors. The combination of two strong schools ensured that the resulting new school was adequately provided with financial resources and facilities. Currently, the school offers majors including die and mould manufacturing technology, product quality supervision and inspection, computer numerical control technology and application, and optometry and glasses manufacturing. In 2017, the total fixed assets of the school amounted to 441.171 million yuan, of which general teaching equipment was valued at 66.23 million yuan, professional teaching equipment 163.22 million yuan, new equipment and other equipment 26.64 million yuan, and teaching equipment per student 103,000 yuan/person. The school has built one four-star centre for training in die and mould design and manufacturing, and one five-star open training centre for computer numerical control.

The school's adequate financial resources and equipment have provided an ideal foundation for the development of the major in die and mould manufacturing technology. For example, this area of manufacturing requires a great number of precision computer numerical control units; the cost of one unit with average precision is around 500,000 yuan. Higher precision requires a greater number of tools in the unit which makes the cost soar to more than 1,000,000 yuan. In the manufacturing industry, dies and moulds need to be made in many shapes. Basic shapes, such as straight-line, oval and square, cannot fulfil the requirements of modern manufacturing. Processing dies and moulds in complex shapes requires that the units be installed with special tools or a particular type of equipment such as an engraving machine which is expensive. Dies and moulds are used to shape metal in stamping and forging operations or to shape plastics, ceramics and composite materials which must be made of steel. Although the manufacturing unit can finish processing with high precision, the delicate final adjustment must be done manually. During training, a great number of steel cubes are therefore needed on which students can practice which is costly for the school. Although various attempts have been made to imitate the human touch in order to control cost without compromised teaching outcomes, the cost is inevitably high.

Given the school's advantageous geographic position and adequate resources, the VET03 die and mould manufacturing major has been selected as the national preferred major and produces a great number of skilled graduates for local and national enterprises (100% employment rate after graduation).

Automobile industry in Fujian

Another typical example of VET involvement is to be found in the automobile industry which has been a foundation industry in China for many years. Since 2002, when China joined the WTO and created an easier environment for the entry of foreign automobile enterprises, an increased number of foreign investors have come to China. In 2009, with more production capacity and government incentives to spur demand, China sold more than 13,500,000 vehicles, overtaking the US to become the biggest car market in the world (China Daily, 2010). Sales climbed to 24,600,000 in 2015 and then 27,800,000 in 2018. This is an industry full of promise. With the growing income of rural residents and the improved infrastructure, rural areas are gradually emerging as an important arena for the automobile industry. In addition, given issues such as global warming, energy security and air pollution, China has been committed to transportation electrification since 2015, identifying New Energy Vehicles as one of ten key future developmental focuses (State Council, 2015).

In Fujian, the traditional pillar industry is manufacturing, while the automobile industry is one of the key areas with potential. The province is located on the south eastern coast, facing Taiwan across the Taiwan Strait. Given its special location, Fujian proposed in 2004 the establishment of the West Bank Economic Zone, which covers the west coast of the Taiwan Strait (including parts of Guangdong and Zhejiang provinces), for socio-economic development. Approved by the State Council, the West Bank Economic Zone has become a major focus for the Fujian province (National Development and Reform Commission, 2011). In 2015, the Fujian Pilot Free Trade Zone was officially launched. The Zone is ideally positioned to build innovative cross-strait cooperation and open up to Taiwan and other overseas investors (State Council, 2015). Within this context, Fujian has attracted investment from Yulon Motor Co., Ltd which is the largest automobile industry in Taiwan. Daimler AG has also established a joint venture with Fujian Motors Group. Although the automobile industry currently only accounts for 2.7% of Fujian's gross industrial output, it is the focus of Fujian's industrial development in the coming ten years. Without baggage from the past, the government intends to expand the scale of industry, promote structural reform and enhance research capacity and innovation, especially in New Energy Vehicles.

VET05 is a secondary vocational school located in Fuzhou city, Fujian province. This school was originally set up as a school to train workers for the defence industry in 1978. Manufacturing for the defence industry includes a great number of procedures essential to modern manufacturing, such as turning, grinding, milling, cold machining, hot working and drilling. The school's background in the defence industry placed great demands on its infrastructure, teaching staff and students, such as achieving the required quality, security and accuracy. The consequent improvement of infrastructures and teaching staff, as well as outstanding graduates, laid the foundation for the school's tradition of focusing on quality. In upholding the tradition of high quality, the school has developed in accordance with major national strategic guidelines and regional economic development. It has established and continuously optimised its structure of majors, offering 19 majors in five major categories such as machinery manufacturing, automobile operation and maintenance, urban rail transit, information technology and economics. For example, in response to the urban subway development plan of Fuzhou, the school set up an urban rail transit operation and urban rail transit vehicle application and maintenance. In the area of industrial transformation and upgrading, the school has added majors such as industrial robot application and maintenance and 3D printing; to catch up with development trends in the automotive industry, it has added several majors, including New Energy Vehicle and marketing for automotive vehicle and accessories.

Given the importance of the automobile industry in Fujian, the school's automobile operation and maintenance major is offered in collaboration with BMW. The German Dual System education model is used as a blueprint, and students alternate between school-based learning and enterprise-level internships. School and enterprise jointly develop training standards and curriculum systems. BMW is responsible for training, assessment, certification of mechanical and electrical teachers and non-technical teachers in schools. The information platform networked with BMW's German headquarters allows the teaching content to be dynamically updated. Timely evaluation and feedback are provided through the information platform, ensuring two-way dynamic interaction throughout the teaching process. Graduates of this training model demonstrate strong orientation, clear career planning and high quality, and can achieve high-quality employment.

Agribusiness in Shandong

China has a long history of farming and a tradition of intensive cultivation, as well as a huge rural population. With less than 10% of the world's arable land,

China has succeeded in producing a quarter of the world's grain and feeding one-fifth of the world's population. Currently, China ranks first in the world in terms of production of commodities such as cereals and cotton. The Chinese government has always placed high priority on the development of agriculture. With China's structural reform and opening up, reform and development in the agricultural industry have been accelerated and deepened. China's 13th Five-Year Plan calls for "agriculture to be the foundation for building a moderately prosperous society in all aspects and to achieve modernization" (State Council, 2016). The plan continues the previous theme of modernisation of the Chinese agricultural sector, introducing improved technology innovation and effective agricultural social service systems. The plan also responses to the food safety issues arising in China in recent years, to concurrently improve the quality, profitability and safety of the sector. Furthermore, the plan intends to implement additional subsidy regimes for low-income farmers, to increase subsidies for agricultural scientific research, to promote the application of mega data in agriculture, and to develop a modern seed industry by supporting seed technology research and development and building seed breeding bases.

VET07 is a secondary vocational school located in Pingdu, Shandong province. Shandong province is a coastal city located in the north of China and is an important economic and agricultural province with a large population. The province's agricultural production has been a leading sector in China for years, with a complete range of crop production, covering grain crops such as wheat and cash crops such as cotton, peanuts, sesame, tobacco, vegetables, temperate zone fruits, tea and flowers. The area ranks first nationwide in terms of its agricultural exports such as cotton and wheat. The peanuts and poultry meat from Shandong account for more than half of the entire country's exports. Pingdu is the largest county-level city in Shandong province. The city's rural population was reported to make up 60% of its total population in 2017 (Pingdu Government, 2018); 18 of its agricultural products are under national protection, such as celery from Majiagou and grapes from Daze Mountain. Normal celery is four yuan per kilo, while celery from Majiagou, (a town in Pingdu) is 40–80 yuan per kilo and the premium celery from Majiagou can reach up to 200 yuan per kilo. In terms of this impressive success and in addition to support from the government, VET has made a great contribution. VET07 school headmaster summarised the approach, saying:

> During the past 30 years, we have been using the Dual System as the keystone, firmly holding the ideas of being rooted in rural areas and serving agriculture, rural areas and farmers. We want to run a good school which can serve and lead the transformation and upgrading of agriculture, rural areas and farmers.

However, thirty years ago, the school did not have sufficient resources (e.g. financial and technical) to realise these goals. Being a vocational school in a remote rural area, the school suffered from a shortage of money and could not offer students practice-based training. It was common for teachers to instruct students to drive a tractor and to grow crops using only the blackboard. In 1988, the school received assistance from the Hanns Seidel Foundation in Germany, which alleviated the shortage of resources faced by the school. The Foundation also introduced a way to systematically organise and modernise agriculture and agricultural vocational education. In the 1990s, based on the thinking of the Dual System, the school and the Foundation developed a model of 'agriculture-school cooperation, work-study combination', emphasising foundation knowledge and practical skills. In the early 21st century, the school gradually evolved into an 'experimental demonstration-incubation training' model, aimed at improving students' comprehensive abilities through the use of various typical work tasks involved in agricultural production and product processing. After 2012, a 'double closed loop, professional cross border' training model was developed. In this student-centred model, teaching and training is organised according to the complete agricultural industry chain. The model not only pays attention to the learning of individual practical skills, but also to the cultivation of comprehensive abilities within the agricultural system. By realising the transformation from mastery of module vocational skills into the cultivation of production and management capabilities, the school serves the needs of regional economic development and keeps VET in the "hearts" of the peasant population.

Developing high-quality vocational education

China's VET has entered a new era and the developmental focus is gradually shifting from scale expansion to the provision of high-quality vocational education and training. This shift is echoed by all headmasters from selected schools and reflected in practice.

VET05 school has a tradition of high-quality teaching. Set up as a school to train workers in the defence industry, the school complies with higher quality standards than other normal vocational schools. It is selective in its students, teachers and courses. For example, strict background checks are conducted for prospective students to ensure high security and trust. The same process is applied to teachers. Additionally, given the importance of the defence industry, most of the teaching staff are recruited from graduates from top universities such as Peking University and Tsinghua University to ensure quality teaching.

In continuing this tradition, several measures have been taken by the current school management with respect to students, teachers, curriculum and enterprises to ensure high quality in its vocational education. These measures start from the entrance examinations students need to sit, as well as the required upper secondary provincial entrance examination. The headmaster told us: "The number of students who want to study in our school far exceeds our enrolment quota. We must have the examination to pick the best students. It is our first step to ensure our teaching quality."

The recruitment of teaching staff is also competitive. Besides the high-quality teaching staff the school has inherited, the current selection criteria are high; the minimum prerequisite for vocational teachers is a bachelor's degree, and currently all of the school's newly recruited teachers have a master's degree.

As pointed out in the last chapter, the Ministry of Education requires vocational teachers to have a teacher's certificate and at least one skills qualification (dual certificate or '1+X' after 2020) as an action plan which is being implemented by the Ministry. The proportion of vocational teachers with dual certificates in the school we visited is 81% which is higher than the benchmark of 50%. Great efforts have been made by the school management, especially by the senior management team, to achieve such a high ratio, and many measures are being implemented. Specifically, since the prerequisite that a minimum three-year work experience for new vocational teachers will not be effective until 2020, most of the newly recruited teachers do not have much work experience. The school therefore requires these newly recruited teachers to work in enterprises for at least three months over a period of three years. Vocational teachers are different from teachers in general education, hence hands-on experience to enrich teachers' understanding of industry is further required.

One of the teachers we interviewed, who had majored in car repairs, told us that he had learnt mostly from textbooks, and could repair a car on blueprint but knew little about how to repair a car in an authentic working environment. He told us that he was unable to locate the car engine on his first day at work because the engine looked totally different to the diagrams in the textbooks he had studied. Although still insufficient, six months of training had significantly deepened his understanding. Working along the entire repair process had extended his vision and had given him a better idea of the industry, thus benefitting his teaching.

Although workplace training is beneficial to teaching, it has been resisted by some vocational teachers who see it as being time-consuming. In comparison to teaching in the classroom about what they have been doing for years, in their opinion, working in enterprises is challenging and not worthwhile. In order to ensure the implementation of this scheme, working in an enterprise has become part of teachers' annual performance appraisal. Anyone not willing to work in an enterprise will not qualify for promotion.

In an effort to enhance vocational teachers' skills level, the school we visited holds a teachers' vocational skills competition every three year throughout the school. This is the first school in Fujian province to hold this kind of competition. The rationale of such a competition is similar to that sending teachers to work in enterprise. The aim is to make sure that all teaching staff are sufficiently skilled to teach their students the practical skills needed. The initial participation in the competition was low as some of the teachers thought it was a waste of time and did not want to be humiliated in front of their colleagues and students. Participation in the competition is now compulsory for all vocational teachers in the school and has also become part of their annual performance appraisal.

Apart from the quality of students and teachers, the curriculum framework and teaching materials are also an important part of teaching, and being up-to-date is of utmost importance. Concerns are frequently raised by teachers, students and employers that what is being taught in the textbooks is not what is being used in the workplace. The time lag is an obvious problem since several years are required from planning to publishing a textbook. The knowledge which was cutting edge initially may be out of date when the textbook is finally published. In order to minimise this gap, the school invites experts in the particular areas, senior technicians and experienced managers to sit on a committee to address this problem. On a regular basis, normally twice a year, the school presents its curriculum framework, teaching plan and teaching materials to committees for comments and improvement. The most common feedback received relates to techniques and machine models which are no longer used, or out-of-date manuals which do not include the new machines used. Teaching materials and related arrangements are adjusted accordingly to ensure that the most recent changes and trends in industry are added to the teaching syllabus.

In addition, so as to enhance teachers' understanding of the needs of industry, the school arranges training for teachers in specific areas, such as car servicing, working in relevant car service companies for a short period every semester. These teachers follow the working schedule as a normal employee, rotating among all positions. The exercise is meaningful for the teachers as they become familiar with the entire working process, while at the same time they are able to summarise and write cases based on what they have learnt during the work as required by the school. For example, more than 200 examples illustrating the structure of the most recent engine models and how to panel beat different car bodies have been accumulated and used as supplementary materials to students' textbooks. These examples are up-to-date and practical, and therefore used to ensure the practicality of the courses.

To further control quality, the school also places high standards for training students who have been selected by companies wishing to recruit them when they graduate from the school. Due to the shortage of skills and well-trained vocational graduates, the students are welcomed by these employers. Most of the graduates sign employment contracts months before graduation. The employment rate among the graduates has been above 98% for many years. In such a context, the school has to rank the companies into groups in terms of their size, capacity and reputation. This is an efficient way of ensuring that the graduates have better chances to secure a good start for their careers, and shows that the school management is very confident in preparing their graduates.

In order to ensure the high quality of students entering, the school holds an extra examination in addition to the normal vocational entry examination; this practice is not common in other schools. The majority of secondary vocational schools in China suffer from low enrolment rates because the preference for academic excellence is deeply rooted and prevalent in the public's mind. However, many students want to be admitted into this school despite the additional examination requirement because of its reputation. One student commented: "The school is well known, its brand is the guarantee of a good job. That is why I want to study here." Its good reputation also brings the school a better chance of cooperating with enterprises. The school has formed a long-term partnership with top 500 companies such as BMW and Benz. With BMW's sponsorship, its BMW Class has adopted the curriculum framework designed by the BMW institute, teaching the latest knowledge, techniques and skills. After graduation, students from this class have the opportunity to work with BMW's subsidiaries and dealers in South China, which is an attractive career pathway for students and a strong motivation for students to study in the school.

Similarly, in VET03, the merger of two schools has brought sufficient finance and infrastructure to provide high-quality education and training. With the support of a China-Japan national technical collaboration project, the school has developed a Modern Moulding Technology Training Centre. The establishment of the Centre has further enhanced the quality of the major in die and mould manufacturing as well as the major in computer numerical control technology and application. According to the agreement between the two governments, the Centre receives technical support from Japan by sending eight long-term experts and 15 short-term experts to the Centre. The long-term experts from Japan reside in the school, providing training for the teachers and short-term experts hold training sessions to update teachers on the latest technology in industry. Every year, the school selects 20 teachers to study die and mould manufacturing technology in Japan. After their return, these teachers are assigned to teach or instruct practical sessions at the Centre. Besides sending teachers to Japan, the school selects students and sends them to study in Japan. This approach is rare among Chinese vocational schools, but it significantly enhances students' skills level and other abilities (e.g. language, communication, sense of independence and team work). In addition, the Japanese counter-partner is also responsible for purchasing equipment (worth 172,000,000 yen) for the Centre and provides financial support (295,000,000 yen). China's contribution is to provide land, facilities and financial support of approximately 23,374,000 yuan. This joint input allows the Centre to be equipped with the most advanced facilities and to have a group of high-quality teaching staff at its disposal. The quality of graduates is high and meets the demand from industry.

Learning from foreign experience

Introducing the Dual System in China's VET

As reviewed in the last chapter, the German VET model emphasises the importance of a close school-enterprise relationship. The level of an enterprise's participation in VET is high and the benefits of proactive participation have been repeatedly justified. German legislation reinforces this cooperation. In China, VET is still at an early stage and is learning from the German experience with ongoing experiments.

VET05 school has formed a partnership with BMW to foster students who will work in BMW's agents and dealers in South China. The school also offers training and re-skilling programmes for employees with BMW China. In order to be admitted into the class sponsored by BMW (called the BMW Class), students who have finished their first two years of study need to sit a selection test overseen by BMW training institution in China. This institute is located in Shanghai and is responsible for all training and development issues in China,

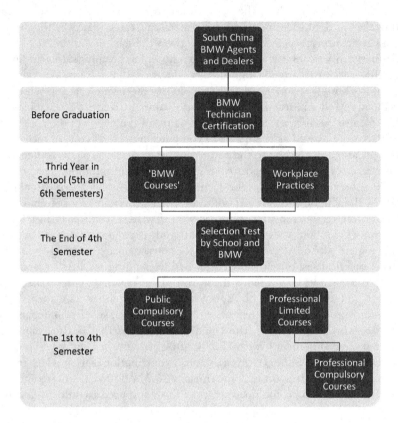

Figure 4.1 BMW Class training system.
Source: Data collected in 2018.

reporting directly to BMW's headquarters in Munich, Germany. The overall BMW Training System is illustrated in Figure 4.1.

For each batch, there are a maximum of 32 students who can be selected for the BMW classes. The number 32 is not randomly selected but is a number which has been assessed carefully and then approved by BMW institution in order to control its training effects and quality. The school has built a training base for BMW, which complies with BMW's global standardised requirements. For example, facilities have carpet flooring and air conditioning; all stock, including nails, are digitalised with bar codes and closely monitored by the institution in Shanghai. All tools are stored consistent with all other BMW training bases in order to ensure that all trainers around the world visiting this training base can find whatever they need. Students are always required to wear uniforms with the BMW logo.

In order to effectively conduct teaching and training activates, the 32 students are divided into two classes. Throughout their one year in the BMW Class, the students' training schedule consists of 40 days of classroom-based teaching in BMW-customised courses (i.e. Term 1) and 3 months of workplace training in BMW enterprises, followed by 40 days in school (i.e. Term 2) and then three months in the workplace. At the end of the year, all students are required to sit BMW's Technician Certification Test. The students who pass the test can choose to join BMW's distributors or agencies in South China.

The materials used during the 40 days' classroom teaching are designed by the BMW headquarters in Germany. The materials are translated by the Shanghai BMW training institution and minor adjustments are made based on the different situations of the various schools, the different skills needed in the region and the different vehicle models sold in the region. The 40 days' teaching is further broken down into different modules. The number of modules increases as the complexity of the contents increases. In order to assess learning outcomes, each mould produced is assessed using a 1000-point system, which is a reflection of strict and accurate quality control by BMW (Figure 4.2 shows an extract of the 1000-point marking sheet for one module).

The BMW Class teachers are selected from the current teachers in the school. However, in order to teach in this class, teachers must be certified by BMW as technical trainers. As with the students in the BMW Class, the training for teachers is long and under close supervision of Shanghai BMW training institution to ensure that these teachers are highly qualified for teaching this class. The training and certification are divided into two stages: the first stage focuses on certification (Figure 4.3) and the second stage focuses on further training and advancement (Figure 4.4).

Furthermore, to ensure consistent teaching and training outcomes, the institution conducts random inspections of the school without giving notice. This approach leaves no time for either school or teachers to prepare for the inspection. In other words, the school and teachers must ensure that they fulfil every single requirement at all times during the partnership. This system places pressure on the school and teachers, and is an incentive for them to maintain high-quality training for its students and teachers.

Certification of BMW trainers can be difficult to obtain, but the reward can be significant. BMW encourages these trainers to teach across different areas, which is a useful way to develop their connections and share their experience. BMW covers all expenses incurred during the teaching visit such as five-star accommodation and other expenses. This gesture is intended to communicate that BMW is a company that highly values skills and knowledge, and is an effective way of promoting its brand and overall reputation.

The cooperation between the school and BMW goes beyond teaching and training of students and teachers in school. The terms of the partnership require the school to provide training and development programmes for current BMW employees. Instead of asking the school to run the programmes, BMW has introduced a marketized competition mechanism. Within BMW's training system, all employees can freely choose to be trained at any BMW training base (i.e. schools like VET05 or any other school that has signed a partnership agreement

1000-points Performance Evaluation Form

Category	Item	Points
Basic Information	Name	
	Module: M1	
	No.	
Professional Ability	New BW 5 senses LI	10
	Identification of instrument panel	10
	Identification and judgement of var	10
	BW Overview	10
	BP Pre-class test	10
	Learning box check	100
	Class task completion	500
	After class task 1	10
	After class task 2	10
	After class task 3	10
	After class task	100
	After class test	100
	Stage assessment	200
Score/Grade	Total score	1000
	Total score after correction	
	Total score after correction	
	Grade	
Professionalism/ Correction factor	Total correction index	Total correction
	Attitude & performance	5
	Cooperation & communication	5
	Punctuality	5
	Safety regulations	5
	Professionalism ethos	5
	Responsibility	5
In-class Task	In-class task total score	250
	Review the previous module	10
	Car development	10
	Domestic sales of car models	10
	The importance of vehicle inspection	10
	Vehicle installation and protection	10
	Vehicle equipment	10
	Communication level	10
	Fluency operation 1	10
	Fluency operation 2	10
	Fluency operation 3	10
	Fluency operation 4	10
	Fluency operation 5	10
	Fluency operation 6	10
	Item report and writing -- (with) score	10

Figure 4.2 1000-point performance evaluation form.
Source: Data collected in 2018.

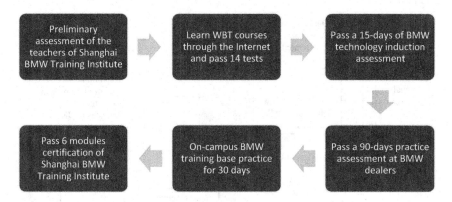

Figure 4.3 BMW certification stage for teachers (trainers).
Source: Data collected in 2018.

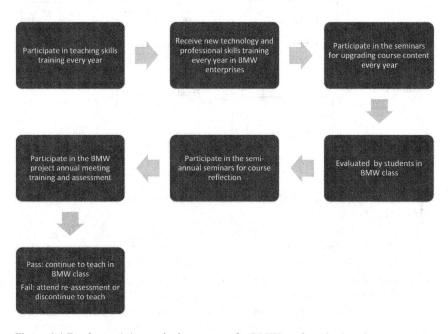

Figure 4.4 Further training and advancement for BMW teachers (trainers).
Source: Data collected in 2018.

with BMW) in China. BMW pays the training base for the training sessions offered which are calculated on the basis of how many sessions are held and how many BMW employees are trained. This system potentially leads to competition between training bases which must deploy their best resources to attract employees to enrol in their sessions. A situation is created where all parties are better off. BMW has its employees well trained for increased productivity, the school is

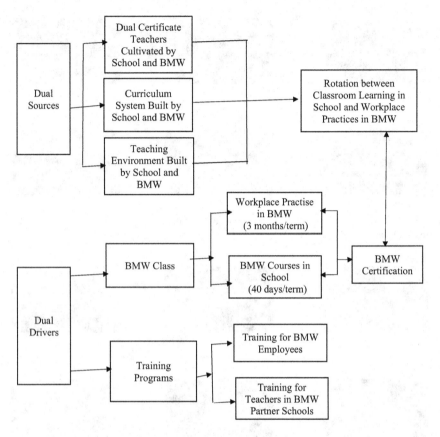

Figure 4.5 Dual source and dual drivers' model in VET05.
Source: Data collected in 2018.

well paid and will invest more in BMW's programmes, and the employees' skills are improved. Thus, the training and development programmes of BMW enter a virtuous cycle from both short-term and long-term perspectives.

To summarise, the model of collaboration between the school and BMW is characterised by 'dual sources' and 'dual drivers' as shown in Figure 4.5. The system is a modified form of the Dual System model used in Germany with the purpose of localising international practices with Chinese characteristics.

Localising of the Dual System in China's VET

The VET07 school was initially funded by the Germany Foundation. In contrast to VET05, VET07 adopted the Dual System nearly 30 years ago (1991–2019) but with even stronger orientation towards localisation.

In 1991, after three years of preparation, the cooperative project between China and Germany was officially launched; it was a well-planned project and was implemented progressively with a long-term view (see Figure 4.6).

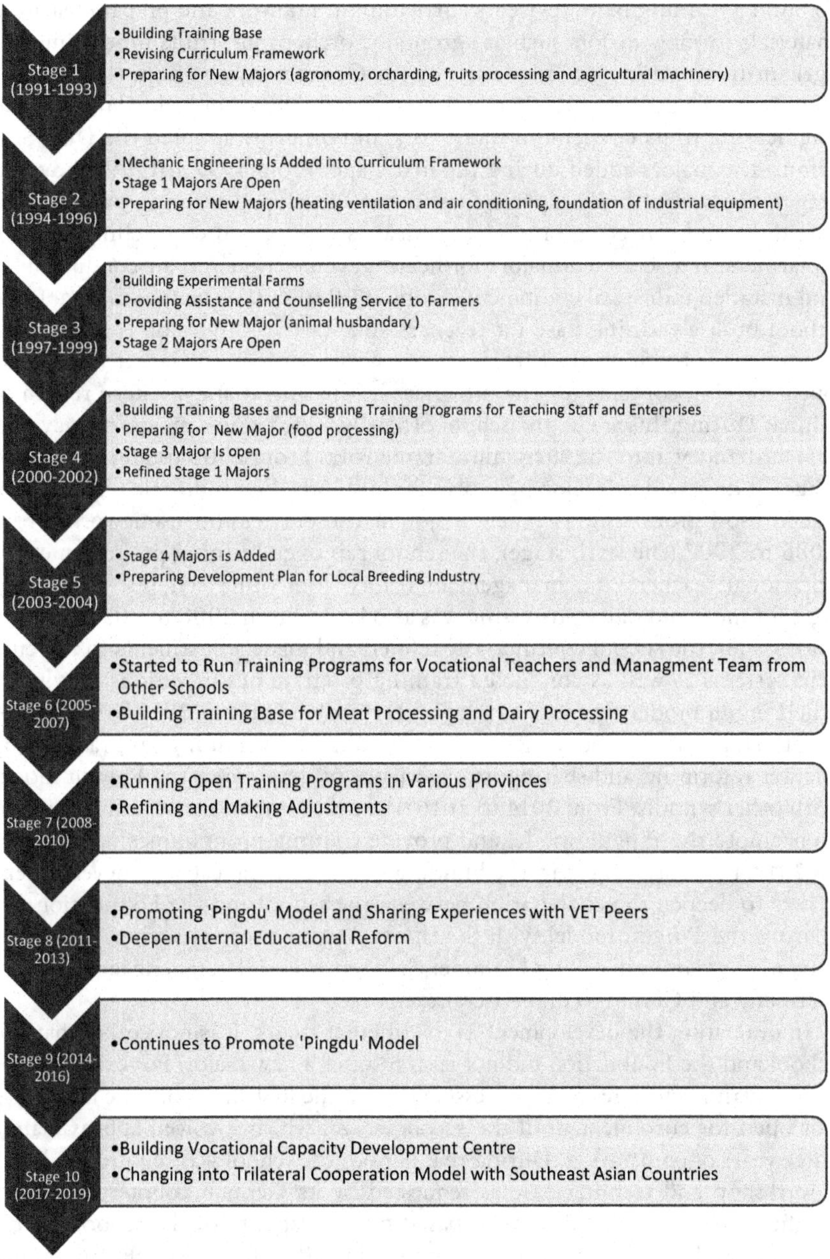

Stage 1 (1991-1993)
- Building Training Base
- Revising Curriculum Framework
- Preparing for New Majors (agronomy, orcharding, fruits processing and agricultural machinery)

Stage 2 (1994-1996)
- Mechanic Engineering Is Added into Curriculum Framework
- Stage 1 Majors Are Open
- Preparing for New Majors (heating ventilation and air conditioning, foundation of industrial equipment)

Stage 3 (1997-1999)
- Building Experimental Farms
- Providing Assistance and Counselling Service to Farmers
- Preparing for New Major (animal husbandary)
- Stage 2 Majors Are Open

Stage 4 (2000-2002)
- Building Training Bases and Designing Training Programs for Teaching Staff and Enterprises
- Preparing for New Major (food processing)
- Stage 3 Major Is open
- Refined Stage 1 Majors

Stage 5 (2003-2004)
- Stage 4 Majors is Added
- Preparing Development Plan for Local Breeding Industry

Stage 6 (2005-2007)
- Started to Run Training Programs for Vocational Teachers and Managment Team from Other Schools
- Building Training Base for Meat Processing and Dairy Processing

Stage 7 (2008-2010)
- Running Open Training Programs in Various Provinces
- Refining and Making Adjustments

Stage 8 (2011-2013)
- Promoting 'Pingdu' Model and Sharing Experiences with VET Peers
- Deepen Internal Educational Reform

Stage 9 (2014-2016)
- Continues to Promote 'Pingdu' Model

Stage 10 (2017-2019)
- Building Vocational Capacity Development Centre
- Changing into Trilateral Cooperation Model with Southeast Asian Countries

Figure 4.6 The 30 years of the Pingdu model.
Source: Data collected in 2018.

The first stage took place from 1991 to1993 during which the school started to build a training base, revise its curriculum framework and prepare teaching materials for new majors such as agronomy, orcharding, fruits processing and agricultural machinery as requested by the German experts from the Foundation. Later, from 1994 to1996 (the second stage), the school added mechanical engineering to its curriculum framework and officially adopted the Dual System to the majors added during the first stage. From 1997 to1999 (the third stage), the school built experimental farms, developed training programmes for adults and started to provide technical assistance and counselling services to farmers. It also added majors for heating, ventilation and air conditioning, and installed industrial equipment. From 2000 to 2002 (the fourth stage), the school built a training base for teachers and started to develop training programmes for teaching staff from other schools and enterprises. It also developed training contents for the provinces in the inland and Western region of China. During this stage, the school officially added a new major, namely animal husbandry, into the curriculum framework. From 2003 to 2004 (the fifth stage), it designed a development plan for local breeding industries. The school added food processing as a new major in the curriculum framework. From 2005 to 2007 (the sixth stage), the school ran open training programmes for vocational teachers and management teams from other schools. A training base for meat and dairy processing was also built. From 2008 to 2010 (the seventh stage), the school continuously refined and made adjustments to the current systems as well as conducted training programmes in various provinces. The Pingdu model emerged as a new 'star' in VET. From 2011 to 2013 (the eighth stage), the school continued to consolidate its training programmes by further reforming and sharing its experience of developing the Pingdu model with other schools. From 2014 to 2016 (the ninth stage), the school continued to promote the Pingdu model and provide training programmes nationwide. In 2017, the tenth stage saw the building of a vocational capacity development centre to deepen the cooperation between the school and the Foundation. By sharing the Pingdu model with Southeast Asian countries such as Laos, Vietnam and Cambodia, Pingdu model changed from bilateral engagement (i.e. Germany and China) to multilateral exchanges.

In evaluating the development in its different stages, it is noticeable that the school and the Foundation did not rush to offer a new major. For example, the school planned to offer fruit processing during the first stage, but the major was not open for enrolment until the second stage, which involved approximately three years of preparation. During that period, the school was required to build a workshop and training base as requested by its German counterpart. After careful evaluation and adjustment based on the capacity of the school's infrastructure and teaching staff, the major was adopted and approved. Furthermore, the majors and courses were developed and closely linked to agricultural production. For example, the school started with majors such as agronomy, orcharding, fruits processing and agricultural machinery, which laid the foundation for agricultural production. Subsequently, the school introduced courses in agricultural engineering in order to catch up with the pace of industrialisation and modernisation in agriculture.

During these 30 years, the introduction of the German model has not been easy. First, based on the German system, the Foundation requested that the school should increase the proportion of students' practice sessions. This request was strongly opposed by students' parents and teachers. Parents thought that practice sessions were worthless and suspected that the school was using their students as cheap labour. Some teachers did not want to follow the instructions of the Foundation, but rather wanted to keep teaching in their own way by following textbooks. This resistance created conflict between the Foundation and the school. Under such pressure, the school made adjustments by promoting teachers who could teach the German syllabus. Furthermore, the school invited experts from Germany to hold workshops and seminars at the school to popularise the German thinking and logic underlying its model. At the same time, the school selected and sent some teachers to Germany for training in order to enhance their understanding of the German model.

Despite increased acceptance and recognition, the school encountered another problem. In accordance with the German Dual System, the school required its second and third year students to work at least four days every week on their family farmland. The four-day requirement was copied from the German VET system in the agricultural sector. There are a great number of family-run farms in Germany, while in Pingdu most of the students and their family only have a few farmlands which are not suitable for students to practice what they learnt in school. The farmlands in Pingdu are spread over a wide area without proper transportation facilities. In addition, none of the residents wanted students to experiment on their farmlands. These aspects attracted criticism from students and their families and led the school and the Foundation to review, rethink and reassess the differences between the German VET model and its applicability in Pingdu.

After identifying and acknowledging the differences between the two systems, the school built three sites, five centres and one base, based on the thinking of the Dual System, covering dairy cow husbandry, pig breeding, cropping, dairy processing, fruit processing, meat processing, pastry making, agriculture machinery and biological techniques. These facilities provided a place for students to practice and have expanded with assistance from local enterprises. A leading VET model has been created, referred to as the 'school in factory, factory in school'. An example of this concept is an electronic appliance company which has been residing in the school for nine years and has built two workshops in the school to serve as a training centre for students to practice. The output from these two workshops has accounted for half of the company's total output. In this collaboration, the school has provided the space and students as semi-skilled workers, while the enterprise has provided the raw materials and mentors. This model has enabled the teaching plan to be aligned with the production plan, the teachers from the school to be connected with the mentors from the enterprise, and the students to be connected with the production system.

Introducing the UK system of Modern Apprenticeship in China's VET

Equally significant and as well-established as the Dual System from Germany, the Modern Apprenticeship system from the UK was also introduced in China's VET schools. VET04 is a successful example in this regard.

VET04 is located in Changshu, Jiangsu province. Jiangsu is a province located on the eastern central coast of China, an important part of the Yangtze Delta economic region. The area is one of the leading provinces in finance, education and technology in China. Historically, Jiangsu had a strong light industry sector, but after 1993, growth of the heavy industry sector accelerated and overtook that of light industry, with a strong production base in machinery and becoming one of the major petrochemical industry bases in China (Yearbook of Jiangsu, 2017). Changshu is a county-level city under the jurisdiction of Suzhou, located in the open region of the Yangtze Delta close to where the Yangtze River flows into the sea. With a long history of more than 5,000 years, Changshu has an excellent ancient cultural image in world terms. However, since the Changshu Economic Development Zone was established, the city has changed its image to a modern industrial city. A total of more than two billion yuan have been invested in infrastructure facilities such as water system, sewage process factories and power generation plants. In 2012, Chery and Jaguar Land Rover announced a 50:50 joint venture as well as a research and development centre in Changshu. In 2018, Chery Jaguar Land Rover signed a new agreement with Changshu to launch a production programme for a New Energy Vehicle. The project involves a total investment of 7,000,000 yuan to make electric vehicles from 2020. The Changshu plant was the first complete vehicle plant outside the UK and has played a pioneering role in the UK-based electric vehicles development strategy.

Following the establishment of Chery Jaguar Land Rover's plant in 2012, the Modern Apprenticeship pilot project was developed by the school and Chery Jaguar Land Rover in 2014. The Modern Apprenticeship model was not based on a uniform training framework – rather each training institution's framework was designed by the national training organisation within the industry based on an evaluation of industry characteristics, job nature and the needs of employers. At the same time, each course in the curriculum framework had its own required standards. Some of the standards were optional and customised based on the needs of the employer. Teachers could design the teaching contents according to these standards. Therefore, each course was tailor-made to meet the needs of the business. The apprentice had to meet all the requirements in the framework to obtain the corresponding qualification certificate.

However, this process did not suit the situation in China's VET schools. In order to localise the content, the British Consulate General invited British industry association experts to tailor a set of relevant curriculum frameworks and teaching plans for the school of VET04, based on the British Modern Apprenticeship requirements and assessment criteria, combining national industry standards with the specific needs of Chery Jaguar Land Rover. The school maintained continuous communication with the British side and by combining the original talent training programme, gradually refined the teaching plan and teaching content, implementing it after passing the British experts' review. At present, the curriculum framework adopted by the school includes: EUC Level 2 Mechatronics Maintenance Technician Capacity Unit, EUC Level 3 Mechatronic Maintenance Technician Capacity Unit, and BTEC Level 3 Technical Theory Knowledge Unit.

During the first three semesters of the programme, apprentices study in the school; the training includes the Ability Units of EUC Level 2 and the basic theory courses for BTEC Level 3. In the fourth and fifth semesters, the training includes the Competency Units of EUC Level 3 (in the enterprise), supplemented by the BTEC Level 3 developmental phase theory courses (see Figure 4.7). After completing the three frameworks, the apprentices are assessed accordingly, and those who pass the assessment receive the corresponding qualification. In addition to the apprenticeship programme, the talent training programme provides other professional courses and professional skills certification training in order to develop the apprentices' comprehensive professional skills. The British Apprenticeship Behavioural Framework has also been adopted to develop apprentices' behavioural norms, sense of responsibility, teamwork and communication skills. In the last semester of the apprenticeship, when the apprentices enter the company for rotation and fixed-position training in Chery Jaguar Land Rover, the school selects a professional teacher to serve as Work Based Learning Manager. Based on the British apprenticeship model, the teacher tracks the training status of every apprentice on a weekly basis and helps the enterprise address any problem raised during the process.

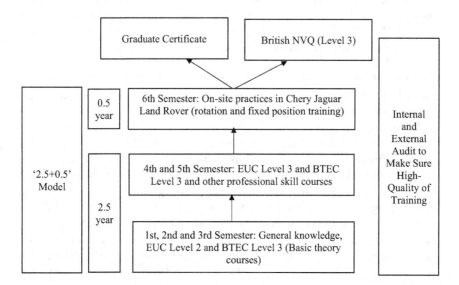

Figure 4.7 Localised apprenticeship in VET04.
Source: Data collected in 2018.

Due to the differences between the Chinese and British education systems, it has been important to prepare a group of Chinese teachers to understand the British apprenticeship system and have relevant professional skills to ensure the success of adopting the new system in the school. From May to June 2014, two qualified training managers from the UK EAL organisation conducted training of the first batch of teachers, evaluators of enterprise engineers and internal auditors in the school. Everyone who participated in the training successfully acquired the qualification certificate for the first phase. The training provided teachers with a preliminary understanding of the British apprenticeship curriculum evaluation system, which laid a good foundation for the next phase of the apprenticeship project.

Following the above-mentioned training in China, the school also sent seven teachers to the UK in August 2014 to participate in training programmes on the British apprenticeship training model and practices. The contents included British apprenticeship teaching philosophy, evaluation methods and other relevant issues. The teachers studied the apprenticeship programme designed by the Warwickshire College and the training programmes designed for Jaguar Land Rover by three well-known training institutions, namely EEF, MGTS and PERA. The teaching implementation process in the UK inspired the teachers significantly, as was illustrated by the comments of one teacher:

> When visiting the Warwickshire College and the EET Technical Training Centre, the instructor of the apprenticeship showed us how to document process data of apprentices. These documents are very standardized and clear. The apprentice's daily training content, training progress, and compliance status are all documented and trackable. In addition, they use very practical and clear TO DO and DONE work cards to label the status and scan the QR code pictures on the wall next to each workbench to obtain learning videos. All of these are efficient and practical.

In 2015 and 2016, the school hired experts from the UK's EAL, REAL and Warwickshire universities to present training workshops which provided the appropriate direction for the implementation of the Modern Apprenticeship model.

The appraisal system of the British apprenticeship model is one of its distinctive features and one of the key reasons for the school introducing this assessment method in its apprenticeship training. After studying the British curriculum standards, the teachers of the school developed a teaching plan and an evaluation plan, and then designed corresponding training programmes and evaluation projects based on the plans. Prior to the training, teachers fully inform the apprentices on the curriculum standard requirements and plans; during the training, teachers closely track the status of apprentices' skills training and communicate with the apprentices in a timely manner; after the training is completed, the apprentices are evaluated with feedback in accordance with the evaluation requirements.

Chery Jaguar Land Rover worked closely with the school during the entire process. The enterprise provided various training programmes for apprentices from the first year of apprenticeship, such as on-the-job training and safety training. Apprentices regularly visited the enterprise to learn about corporate culture, health and safety, lean systems, and workshop production processes and job requirements. The enterprise assigned engineers to teach at the school and appraise apprentices, as well as train school teachers.

Hence, the case of VET04 is an example of a school's efforts to localise a foreign model through modification and adjustment. Along the adoption process, the school also learnt unique lessons regarding ongoing reform and innovation momentum, and explored a foreign apprenticeship model with Chinese characteristics that are suitable for development in China.

Introducing the Japanese Toyota system in China's VET

Besides the VET models from Germany and the UK, some vocational schools in China formed a partnership with Japanese enterprises such as Toyota. The case of VET06, located in Guangzhou city, Guangdong province, is an example of a school working closely with Toyota, incorporating the Toyota system into their operation.

Guangdong is a province in South China and one of the leading provinces driving economic reform and the open-door policy in China since the 1980s. Guangdong Free Trade Zone was launched in 2015. Approved by the State Council, this Free Trade Zone in Guangdong was intended to include Hong Kong and Macau with a view to further opening up the Chinese economy to the world. Efforts have been made to develop the Free Trade Zone into a Guangdong-Hong Kong-Macau cooperation region. By giving Guangdong autonomy in its reforms and economic restructuring initiatives, it is expected that by 2020, Guangdong, together with Hong Kong and Macau, will become one of the most globally competitive and vigorous metropolitan areas in the Asia-Pacific region, and a centre with advanced manufacturing and modern service industries. Guangzhou is the main manufacturing hub of Guangdong province and is home to one of the top three automobile manufacturing bases in China (State Council, 2015). In 2018, the Guangzhou government officially issued the 2025 strategy for the Guangzhou automobile industry. According to the strategy, the Guangzhou government strives to be the leader in vehicle output and sales among the Chinese automobile manufacturing bases with production capacity of up to 5,000,000 units per year (Guangdong Government, 2018).

Against this background, a joint venture between Guangzhou Automobile Industry Group and Toyota Motor was established in 2004, with headquarters in Guangzhou. In the same year, the VET06 school was chosen by Toyota to launch the T-TEP (Toyota Technical Education Program).

Automobile repair and maintenance were the school's traditional strength since it was first established. The introduction of the T-TEP enhanced further integration and improved the advanced vehicle maintenance teaching system. As with other advanced VET models, the T-TEP started with training for a small group of vocational teachers in the school who attended training sessions held by Toyota. After receiving qualifications from Toyota, these teachers were allowed to teach in the Toyota Class. The training session for teachers was conducted on a continuous basis. The school selected teachers and sent them to be trained at Toyota Headquarters in Japan to ensure that these vocational teachers received the most updated training and were aware of the latest techniques at Toyota. The school was also supported by Toyota with regard to training equipment to ensure that students and teachers were trained on all car models sold in the local markets.

During the first year of the T-TEP, students were required to complete academic foundation and professional foundation courses. At the beginning of the second year, the school and Toyota set up a Toyota Class. The students took the core courses in their original class and used the spare time to study the Toyota TEAM 21 (Toyota Education for Automotive Mastery in 21st century) Level 1 course. At the end of the second year, Toyota Day was arranged for students to join a Toyota dealership for internship practice. In the third year, top students were recommended by the dealer and selected to attend an intermediate class to learn further with the Toyota TEAM 21 Level 2 courses, while the rest of the students continued to learn in the Level 1 course. Students who passed the Level 1 assessment could be employed as Toyota Technicians and those who passed the Level 1 and 2 assessments could be employed as Toyota Pro Technicians at a Toyota dealership (see Figure 4.8).

The size of the Toyota Class was limited to 20–25 students and the grouping was four students per car and two students per assembly bench. The courses were taught systematically, following real work practices. Teaching started with car maintenance courses, followed by overhaul system diagnosis, and then comprehensive diagnosis, in line with professional development and integrated with real production systems at Toyota. In addition, during the classes, students were guided by a series of tasks focused on learning independently and cultivating their comprehensive professional abilities.

In addition, Toyota's culture emphasised continuous improvement and attention to detail, from technical to managerial levels. Toyota established a specialised operation and management function, the T-TEP Affairs Bureau. This bureau was responsible for project selection, course introduction, student skill level certification, employment management, project culture construction, convening T-TEP liaison meetings, teacher training and developing a detailed evaluation mechanism for the project. The curriculum framework consisted of various courses and specific requirements for each job category (i.e. general technicians, service advisors or body and paint technicians) and each skill level within each position. The TEAM 21 training courses were designed for general technicians and could be further divided into four levels. The most basic level was called Toyota Technician, and at this level, the students were trained to perform periodic maintenance within a flat-rate time. The next level was called Pro Technician,

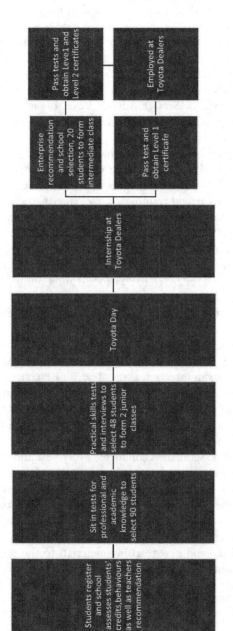

Figure 4.8 T-TEP training process.
Source: Data collected in 2018.

and at this level, the students could perform frequent repair tasks within a flat-rate time. The third level was called Diagnostic Technician, and at this level, the students were trained to perform basic diagnostic procedures for solving individual system problem. The most advanced level was called Diagnostic Master Technician at which the students were able to perform advanced diagnostic procedures for cross-system problem.

TEAM 21 was designed for general technicians, while training courses of the TSA 21 (Toyota Service Advisor Program) were aimed at students who wanted to work as service advisors. Service Advisor Level 1 was designed to train students to perform maintenance and provide repair advice, control service operations and customer follow-up. Service Advisor Level 2 was designed for students who wanted to be trained in complaints handling and all customer requests. In addition, all students who want to be service advisors attend training courses for car body damage assessment. Students who want to be body and paint technicians are required to attend training courses such as the B&P TEAM (Body and Paint TEAM). As with other training courses offered, this course is divided into three levels: B&P Toyota Technician to perform light damage repairs, B&P Toyota Pro Technician to perform medium damage repairs, and B&P Toyota Mater Technician to perform heavy damage repairs and quality control checks.

Toyota's project is not restricted to classrooms and training at the workplace; it extends to a series of activities designed to prepare students for their careers. For example, the school and Toyota create an environment within the Toyota Class for students to learn about brand concepts and enhance brand awareness. Extracurricular activities effectively direct students' reactions, enhance their sense of teamwork and effort, integrate employment education into daily teaching activities and train students in interview skills. The T-TEP Careers Day is organised regularly and provides an opportunity for students to communicate with dealers face-to-face and join the Toyota dealers based on their willingness and the requirements of different dealers. The T-TEP Seminar is one of the key activities aimed at providing the same level of education to students across all T-TEP vocational institutions. The seminar is conducted every year and serves as a platform for understanding the current status of automobile industry development. The most recent topics have included electric vehicles, hydrogen-powered vehicles and plug-in hybrid electric vehicles. The seminar covers and compares these New Energy Vehicles, and emphasises their importance and necessity.

The above cooperation has brought an advanced foreign training system, new ideas, new technology and new teaching materials to the school. The school's education and teaching reforms have thus been effectively supported and professional teaching standards and teaching quality improved.

Engagement with industry: school-enterprise cooperation

There are a great number of enterprises in China which do not have sufficient resources to run sponsorship classes (e.g. BMW Classes or Toyota Classes). In addition to these sponsored classes, another type of cooperation model between schools and small- and medium-sized companies has been widely adopted and has proven successful. For example, in VET05, a partnership was formed between the school and an animation production company, called the Dual Workshops. The school set up a studio at the campus for the company as a production workshop and the company provided workshop spaces for students to work in the company. In contrast to the common practice of sending third year students to work in companies, the Dual Workshops started from the second year.

The school's studio serves as a production unit for the company. The company assigns a production executive to the studio to oversee production, and the executive is responsible for providing training to the teachers and ensuring consistent production quality. Throughout the year, the teachers and students work on commercial projects from the company. For example, animation production normally involves a great amount of drawing and it is cost-efficient for the company to get students to draw them frame by frame. Teachers provide assistance to students' drawings and make on-the-spot corrections. In addition to drawing routines, animation production also involves other processes such as drawing storyboard, lighting, compositing, music and sound design, and colour grading, which require comprehensive studio facilities available in the company. Hence, after learning at the campus studio, students spend their summer and winter vacations in the company workshop to learn the rest of the production steps. In contrast with submitting a project for grading, working as a team member in a real workplace enhances the employability of students, offering them a better way to gain the skills required in most workplaces.

In other VET schools, such as VET06 and VET08, schools and partner companies have jointly developed a training plan and courses. Unlike large companies which are able to introduce a comprehensive curriculum system, these small- and medium-sized companies can only add a few core courses to the original curriculum. These courses are taught by experts from these companies. The assessment of the courses is also carried out by the companies. At the end of the course, the companies assess the performance of students and provide grades. At the same time, depending on the teaching needs of the curriculum, the school also assigns teachers to the enterprises for theory teaching and managing students. In this process, the school teachers are treated as employees of these companies. Students alternate working in the enterprises with studying at school. Upon graduation, students have priority in choosing to work in these companies.

In comparison with large-sized companies such as BMW and Toyota, the school-enterprise cooperation between vocational schools and small- and medium-sized companies is relatively loose. During our interviews, the managers from small- and medium-sized companies expressed concerns about the insufficient capital and facilities to support vocational school training. The priority is to utilise every available resource for production to survive in fierce competition. Sometimes these companies are forced to withdraw money and resources invested in vocational schools in order to expand their production. Investment in vocational education and training is also a long-term process which might take years to become effective. In the case of small companies, the managers are concerned as to whether they can still run the same business in the long run and whether they can retain their skilled workers.

Concluding remarks

In this chapter, we presented a number of VET schools as case studies with the focus on alignment with economic and industrial development, improving the quality of VET schools, learning from foreign experience, and developing strong connections between VET schools and industries/enterprises. These case studies demonstrate that great efforts have been made to introduce internationally well-established VET models and then localise them according to the situation in China. However, in comparison with Germany, the UK and Japan, China's VET needs more attention and assistance from all levels of governments and other stakeholders (e.g. industries and enterprises). Other important issues which need to be addressed include areas related to improving the school management system, ongoing reform of curriculum and teaching materials, upgrading knowledge and skills of teaching staff and enhancing students' learning experience and potential career development. These issues will be the key themes in the following chapter.

References

China Daily, 2010. Chinese auto market takes over US as world's largest [online] http://www.chinadaily.com.cn Available at http://www.chinadaily.com.cn/china/2010-01/09/content_9291861.htm [accessed on 21 February 2019]

Guangdong Government, 2018. Notice of the general office of Guangzhou municipal government on printing and distributing Guangzhou's deepening of the 'internet + advanced manufacturing industry' action plan [online] http://www.gz.gov.cn Available at http://www.gz.gov.cn/gzgov/s2812/201901/b7766de309aa42d3bb96fde9f f545df0.shtml [accessed on 20 February 2019]

Gülseçen, S. and Kubat, A., 2006. Teaching ICT to teacher candidates using PBL: A qualitative and quantitative evaluation. *Journal of Educational Technology & Society*, 9(2), pp. 96–106.

National Development and Reform Commission, 2011. Development planning of the economic zone on the west bank of the Taiwan Straits [online] http://www.ndrc.gov.cn Available at http://images.mofcom.gov.cn/aetats/accessory/201104/130258 6821858.pdf [accessed on 21 February 2019]

Pingdu Government, 2018. Statistical bulletin of national economic and social development of Pingdu City in 2017 [online] http://www.pingdu.gov.cn Available at http://www.pingdu.gov.cn/n2/n687/n689/n701/180404092937382411.html [accessed on 25 February 2019]

Stake, R. E., 1995. *The art of case study: Perspective in practice research.* London: Sage.

State Council, 1980. The 6th five-year plan for national economic and social development of the People's Republic of China (Abstract) [online] www.gov.cn Available at: http://www.ndrc.gov.cn/fzgggz/fzgh/ghwb/gjjh/200506/W020050715581805733448.pdf [accessed on 22 February 2019]

State Council, 2015. The implementation suggestions from department of transportation on the promotion and application of new energy vehicles in transportation industry [online] www.gov.cn Available at http://www.gov.cn/gongbao/content/2015/content_2883248.htm [accessed on 21 February 2019]

State Council, 2015. The overall plan for China (Fujian) free trade pilot are [online] www.gov.cn Available at http://www.gov.cn/zhengce/content/2015-04/20/content_9633.htm [accessed on 21 February 2019]

State Council, 2015. The overall plan for China (Guangdong) free trade pilot area [online] www.gov.cn Available at http://www.gov.cn/zhengce/content/2015-04/20/content_9623.htm [accessed on 20 February 2019]

State Council, 2016. The 13th five-year plan for national strategic emerging industries development [online] www.gov.cn Available at http://www.gov.cn/zhengce/content/2016-12/19/content_5150090.htm [accessed on 25 February 2019]

Yearbook of Jiangsu, 2017. [online] http://www.cnki.net Available at http://tongji.cnki.net/kns55/Navi/YearBook.aspx?id=N2017110026&floor=1### [accessed on 27 February 2019]

Yearbook of Shanghai, 2017. [online] http://www.shanghai.gov.cn Available at http://www.shanghai.gov.cn/nw2/nw2314/nw24651/nw43437/index.html [accessed on 21 February 2019]

Yin, R., 1984. *Case study research: Design and methods.* Beverly Hills: Sage.

5 Reforming the VET system and enhancing teachers' and students' career development

Introduction

VET is closely related to national and regional economic development. During the process of promoting new industrialisation, government, industries, enterprises and educators tend to pay more attention to the development of VET. At the same time, efforts are made to promote institutional reform and deepen educational reform, such as encouraging ongoing curriculum development, strategic transition and reform of the VET system, as well as upgrading the school management system.

Some fundamental underpinning concepts have changed regarding the development of VET in China in recent years with the introduction of well-established VET models and the involvement of foreign enterprises. For example, the central themes of VET development have changed from emphasising being 'ability-based' as a single core element to combining this element with being 'student-oriented' as a dual core element. Abilities are no longer defined narrowly as abilities and skills for particular job positions, but include broader concepts such as professionalism, behaviour, logical thinking, communication, teamwork, potential for further study, career development and practical abilities. With regard to being student-oriented, the process of learning is the process of interaction between teachers and students with orientation towards students' capability development and overall learning satisfaction. Learning is a process in which students actively obtain knowledge, form abilities, adjust attitudes and are able to be employed in a relevant field.

We will elaborate the relevant issues in this chapter. First, we will describe the educational reforms implemented in vocational schools to serve national and regional development as well as take students' interests and needs into consideration. The details discussed include ongoing curriculum development, building pathways between VET and general academic education, strategic transition of vocational schooling, taking responsibility in society and the community, and sharing the experience of VET reform domestically and internationally. Second, we will focus on the issue of teachers' development by discussing the recent efforts made by schools and teachers themselves to improve their knowledge, skills and teaching capabilities in order to achieve a better student learning experience. Third, we will elaborate the efforts being made to cultivate students' abilities, skills and professionalism as well as develop students' potential careers, thus placing students at the centre of VET.

Reforming China's VET

Ongoing curriculum development

The curriculum applied in general education is designed around academic knowledge with minor variations. However, in the VET sector, curriculum development is influenced by various factors and becomes more diverse. The curriculum needs to respond to rapid changes in the labour market, ongoing changes in local industries as well as follow the reform agenda of economic development nationally and regionally.

For example, VET01 school only offers four to five majors which vary every year. In 2015, the high star-rated majors were hotel operation and management, Chinese cooking and nutrition, business English and e-commerce. In 2016, the high star-rated majors offered were hotel operation and management, Chinese cooking and nutrition, foreign languages for tourism (including English, Japanese and Korean) and visa application processing, and city urban rail transit. The choice of majors reflects the school's sensitivity to external changes and the skills needed in the labour market. Since 2014, China's e-commerce has witnessed a dramatic rise in online micro-stores (China Daily, 2018). This growth changes the purchase and consumption behaviours and habits of consumers. A core course on design of online micro-stores was added to the school's curriculum framework of its e-commerce major.

VET03 school, located in Shanghai, is another interesting example. Since economic reform in the 1970s, Shanghai has achieved a rapid and sustained growth. The city's manufacturing industry has long played a supporting and driving role in its economy, with famous brands such as Forever and Phoenix Bicycle, Shanghai Watch, Huili Shoes, Seagull Shampoo and Butterfly Sewing Machine. At the time, these were the 'three big things' to which the majority aspired and which symbolised material success – a sewing machine ('flying-man' in Shanghai), a watch ('Shanghai' from Shanghai watch company) and a bicycle ('forever' and 'phoenix' are both from Shanghai). The Shanghai brands dominated the 'big things' and 'Made in Shanghai' was the synonym of 'superior quality'.

However, with the rise of technology such as quartz movement and the appearance of luxury watch brands, the local watchmaking industry experienced difficulties. The school major for watchmaking was removed from the curriculum in 2000 due to the sharply shrinking market needs. With the improvement of people's living standards in recent decades, mechanical watches, especially high-end watches, have re-emerged as highly sought-after goods. In order to rebuild Shanghai's watchmaking industry, it was important to develop its own technicians. In addition, imported watches require high maintenance with relatively high costs, which generates employment opportunities for well-trained repair technicians. After an absence of ten years, the major for watch repair and maintenance was reintroduced in schools.

Fujian province is another significant example of the role of VET. In 2008, the Fujian government submitted a proposal to the National Development and Reform Commission for the construction of Fujian's metro system. After two years of planning and evaluating, Line 1 and Line 2 were approved by the State Council (Xinhua, 2017). Expectations were that there would be a demand for skilled workers and technicians in urban rail transit. The construction of these metro lines may have taken three to five years and it would have been too late to set up urban rail transit majors after the construction had been completed. Within this context, the school management in VET05 submitted a plan to the Department of Education in Fujian province, offering a new urban rail transit programme with two majors – one for urban rail transit operation management such as conductors and the other for vehicle applications, maintenance and repairs. Initially, Fujian Metro's plan was to recruit its employees from tertiary vocational education institutions, not from secondary vocational school, based on the rationale that students with tertiary vocational background are more skilful. However, one important factor was ignored, namely, demand was for employees with middle-level skills, while tertiary vocational students may have proven to be overqualified for the job requirements. This mismatch was later verified, as few tertiary vocational students applied for metro jobs. Eventually, VET05 received approval to provide its training programme. The school was the first and only secondary vocational school offering this programme in Fujian province. The employment rate of students graduating from this programme has been nearly 100% in recent years.

Other reform models have been adopted by schools; for instance, VET07 developed its curriculum framework based on the concept of simplification. This framework was developed over several stages. Initially, courses covered all skills and knowledge needed in agriculture; subsequently, the school made a bold move and streamlined the traditional framework centred on majors by breaking the traditional boundary between majors. For example, instead of offering around ten courses covering foundation and professional subjects in agricultural engineering, the school restructured these courses into the four subjects of professional theory, professional calculation, professional drafting and professional practice. Students had more time to practice, thus remaining consistent with the goals of achieving a useful learning experience. The school also encouraged students to learn about upstream and downstream courses or cross-principle courses once they had completed the initial courses. For example, students who majored in fruit processing could go upstream to learn how to plant and prune fruit trees and perform soil analysis, or go downstream to learn about fruit storage and marketing.

Building pathways between VET and general academic education

In the past, the options for vocational graduates in China to further their studies into generally academic-oriented education were limited. Advocacy from educators has led to policies and efforts increasingly contributing to building a

VET system in China, with models such as '3+2' and '3+4' models, which enable vocational students to access pathways to other academic tertiary education institutions.

An example of the above-mentioned models is the die and mould manufacturing course offered in VET03 based on a '3+4' vocational education model which intends to build a link between secondary vocational education and tertiary education. The '3' refers to the three years studying in secondary vocational schools and the '4' refers to the four years studying at university. The new model provides students a pathway to enter university, restructuring the curriculum framework to ensure a smooth transition from secondary vocational education to tertiary vocational education. VET03 and its partner university jointly discussed and formulated a pilot plan for the new model with the aim of aligning the original curriculum system of the secondary vocational school with the university's undergraduate programmes. The new model can be seen as an integrated system which includes a professional core curriculum module with a literacy improvement module, as well as a professional skills training module.

The new model adopted the concept of 'three teachers and three bases' (see Figure 5.1). The 'three teachers' refer to secondary vocational teachers, university teachers and enterprise mentors; the 'three bases' refer to the three training bases of secondary vocational schools, enterprises and universities. The first batch of 40 students completed their studies at the school and the position rotation training within the enterprise in 2017. The students then sat examinations organised by the Municipal Commission of Education in Shanghai and the skills level test organised by the partner university; all were admitted to the university.

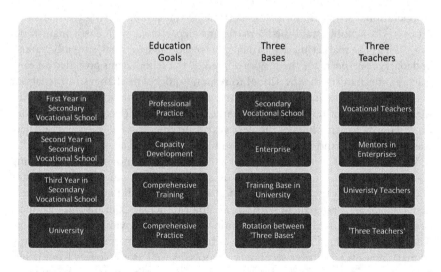

Figure 5.1 '3+4' model in VET03.
Source: Data collected in 2018.

Strategic transition of vocational schooling

Vocational schools are experiencing a rapid transition in China. Some schools are transitioning their schooling according to the changes in regional industrial structure, some are transitioning in order to provide community training as a reflection of the shift of national policy as well as rationalisation of educational resources, and others are transitioning from general education (i.e. upper secondary school) to vocational education in order to fulfil specific development requirements. During their transition, these schools demonstrate distinctive features with different purposes.

VET02, for instance, offers 12 majors with the focus on IT development, including courses in digital media technology applications, computer network technology, software and information services, numerical control technology applications, electrical operations and control, and electromechanical technology applications (robot application and maintenance). However, the school was originally founded as a chemical engineering vocational school under the Ministry of Chemical Industry. In the 1990s, a survey conducted in Shanghai showed that only a total of 59 graduates were recruited from this school over a period of five years, indicating a drastic decrease caused by Shanghai's industrial upgrading for further development in the 1990s when chemical factories with high energy consumption and high pollution were required to relocate to remote suburbs. Consequently, the school management decided that the school needed to respond to the changes and act quickly. The school collected data indicating that the IT industry in Shanghai had grown by 36% annually, which was significantly higher than the average GDP growth. This development meant that the IT area would lead to a large increase in demand in the job market. The school management decided to develop IT programmes as its core focus and adjusted its operational structure to realise its strategic transition. During the transition process, the school established a marketing department with three main functions. First, the marketing department was responsible for analysing job markets and market prospects for the majors offered by the school, thus provided an early warning mechanism for the school to respond quickly to changes in the labour market. Second, the marketing department was responsible for student employment recommendations. Third, the marketing department provided suggestions on the quota for enrolments the next year. Enrolments were open only if there was potential demand for certain skills in the labour market.

VET01 presents another example of a transition path, moving from providing vocational education to students to providing training to employees in industry and residents from the community. In 2017, the school did not take in any students due to an arrangement with the Beijing Municipal Commission of Education to shift the school's role from training students to providing social training. The school developed and ran a series of training programmes for teachers from primary schools and lower secondary schools, as well as employees from enterprises and residents from local communities. The training programmes covered topics from enhancing professionalism and improving daily life skills (as shown in Figure 5.2). For example, in November 2017, the school was entrusted by the

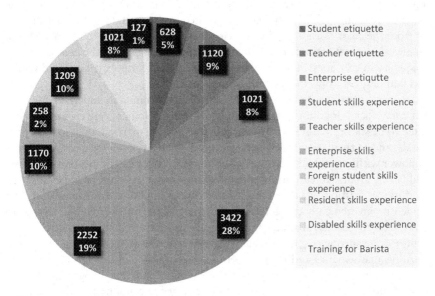

Figure 5.2 Training programmes for community service in 2017 (total: 11,326 students).
Source: 2017 VET01 school's quality report.

Xicheng District Education Committee to conduct a two-phase training event for the secretaries and directors of all the street/neighbourhood communities in Xicheng District; secretaries and directors of 261 communities participated. The school provided a senior etiquette trainer to teach workplace etiquette and communication skills using vivid community work cases. This training left a deep impression on the community cadres. As part of these courses, the school also arranged activities such as cupcake baking, chocolate making and wine tasting. The programmes were highly praised by the participants who commented that the programmes had improved the quality of life of community members. By the end of 2017, the training programmes had been attended by 11,326 people. The number of cadres and staff involved had increased by 120% and the number of community residents had increased from 908 to 1,209 by 2017, an increase of 33%. The school recorded a profit of RMB 1,500,000.

VET08 demonstrates a different transition path. It was founded in 1909 as a general upper secondary school and developed into a vocational school for female students in 1981. It is located in Chongqing which is a major city in Southwest China, one of China's four municipalities under the direct administration of the central government. The establishment of the Chongqing municipality in 1997 represented an initiative of the central government to speed up economic development in the central and western regions. In 2013, the 'One Belt, One Road' initiative was unveiled. In 2014, the Chongqing municipal government issued its Opinions on Implementing the National Strategy of 'One Belt, One Road' to enhance the area's connectivity and influence, and further reinforce its strategic position as a national logistic hub, financial centre and education centre (China Daily, 2014). Unlike the other three municipalities, Chongqing is located in the central and western interior, far from the coast. Although the municipality's area is 13 times greater than that of Shanghai, the vast majority of Chongqing is rural, giving rise to the issue of gender inequality in education. This issue has been a concern for policymakers, educators and families, not only in China but around the world.

Due to the influence of traditional culture, most women in imperial China did not enjoy social or political status with equal rights. Women were raised and educated to be subordinates to their fathers before getting married, then to their husbands, and to their sons if they were widowed. Women possessed a certain degree of power within the family; however, this power did not extend beyond the home and family affairs. In education, textbooks and daily classroom practices contributed to the creation of a set of gender stereotypes in China. For example, female students were generally characterised as being passive, introverted and lacking in space handling skills, abstract thinking and creativity. When these 'labels' were applied to academic studies, female students were regarded as lacking interest in learning mathematics and physics, being more suited to studying literature and foreign languages. In addition, other factors such as poverty, geographical isolation, minority status, disability and early marriage were among the obstacles that prevented women from participating in and completing their education.

In order to improve young women's employment opportunities, VET08 developed its unique programmes aimed at 'fostering elite females for China' with the purpose of developing modern women with relevant knowledge and skills. Based on its curriculum system, the school established four departments with a focus on key training areas, namely training pre-school education teachers, beauty and care services, tourism and finance. The school offered 20 majors in total, including bilingual pre-school education, digital arts and design, secretarial skills, modelling, tourism management and services, hotel management, logistics management and flight attendant training. Although most of the majors and courses were in the humanities, they differed from stereotyped courses which stressed women's lack of interest in learning sciences, and rather developed women's communication skills and good appreciation of arts and beauty based on women's personal and career interests. In addition to its professional curriculum framework, the school also offered sessions to promote beauty and poetic sense of traditional Chinese culture such as calligraphy, flower arrangement, Chinese papercutting, tea art, seal cutting, music performances with traditional Chinese instruments and Tai Chi. Combined with traditional celebrations such as the lantern festival, dragon boat festival and mid-autumn day festivities, the traditional arts, traditional culture and Chinese classics could be integrated within the training programmes, thus cultivating classical cultural heritage within a modern education.

Taking responsibility for society and community

Serving national and regional economic development has been one of the focuses in VET. In addition to cultivating skilled workers, VET schools have started to shoulder responsibility for the overall well-being of community and society.

For example, VET07 school 'incubated' 2,186 family-run farms, plants and agricultural product processing factories. Currently, economic and cultural development between urban and rural areas is in disparity. The central and local governments want to improve the income level for farmers and alleviate their burden, as well as increase the quality of cultural life and safeguard farmers' rights. In order to develop agricultural business, government plans include: (1) increasing the marketisation level of agricultural production and operations, and stabilising the prices of agricultural products; (2) changing the situation of smallholder economic agriculture; (3) achieving economies of scale of agricultural production and operations, and guaranteeing food security.

In Pingdu, these incubated farms, plants and factories provide a feasible solution to address the above-mentioned issues. In contrast to traditional vocational schools which focus on cultivating vocational students, the school in Pingdu focuses on providing vocational training to farmers or vocational farmers. In the past years, the school has produced 55,000 graduates who have become the new force in promoting transformation and developing modern agribusiness. The school has also trained 1,876 owners of family farms and 9,400 individual farmers, as well as provided assistance to establish family farms for its graduates and farmers. The family farm has been the new agricultural corporate entity, using family members as the main labour force, engaging in large-scale professional farming activities, and treating agricultural profit as the family's main source of income. One of the school's graduates, for instance, wanted to establish a wine company and took his research and development team to the school to learn wine production techniques. The school also sent teachers to provide guidance on production and production scale expansion. After several years, the company developed other businesses including grape planting, brewing, research and development, and wine tourism.

Besides providing advice to specific companies, the school also provides counselling services to farmers and teaches agricultural techniques to concerns across the city. For example, the school has collaborated with the local TV channel and has produced a programme which shares advanced techniques adopted by German experts (e.g. 'Green Agriculture' and 'Modern Agriculture') and experiences in production.

In Pingdu, the value chain of production has developed as a 'closed loop'. For instance, in the dairy sector, initially there were no more than 40 dairy cows in Pingdu. In 1998, the school started offering students and farmers a range of subjects from breeding, purchasing, training, milking and preventing diseases – topics teachers had learnt from German experts. Currently, 90% of workers within the dairy sector in Pingdu have received training from the school. Among the school's graduates, 17 have become demonstration farmers. The school's offering is not limited to training; it also provides counselling services to dairy farmers. The students and teachers actively participate in the 'closed loop', design and construction of cow plants, breeding, purchasing, cultivation, quality control and sales for farmers. As one teacher said, "We are very close to the farmers. Our students and teachers know well who has cows and what they need." From the initial 40 cows, there are more than 20,000 cows in

Figure 5.3 Breeding base with a complete value chain.
Source: Data collected in 2018.

Pingdu today. Dairy and husbandry are becoming one of the pillar industries. Since the development is based on the concept of the 'closed loop' (as shown in Figure 5.3), a complete value chain emerges as the outcome.

Another benefit of having this 'closed loop' concept is that the students can learn all units within the loop. The process of learning is the process of production. For example, animal husbandry starts with building barns and continues to breeding and feeding practices, disease prevention, meat processing, quality control and after-sales service. The loop becomes the base line for students either to work as employees or run a business in this sector, which can be meaningful for promoting a modern agribusiness development in Pingdu.

In contrast to VET07's experience, VET03's responsibility is directed at the local community. The school has built a watch culture science museum. It is the first science exhibition pavilion in Shanghai with the theme of timepieces, integrating the history and culture of watches, art display, and education and training. The exhibition area of the museum is about 1,800 square metres, extending over three floors. The first floor consists of the reception hall, multifunction hall and cinema. The second floor houses the ancient Chinese chronograph display area, the European watch display area, the multimedia experience area and the library. The third floor is dedicated to Shanghai's brand watch display area, China watch brand display area, the watch repair tool display area and the watch repair experience centre. The museum has become a place to which citizens and watch lovers are willing to travel from far to visit, and a place for watch culture promotion and watch science education. In addition, the watch repair major at the school admits people with disabilities. Due to the relatively low requirements of mobility and practicality, it is feasible and helpful for people with disabilities to be re-skilled and re-establish their lives through this pathway.

Sharing the experience of VET reform domestically and internationally

Given the rapid development of the VET system in China in recent years, other schools in China and abroad want to learn from the experience of successful VET schools. These schools are sharing their experiences with schools in remote rural areas in China as well as with other countries, in particular China's neighbouring countries in Asia.

Xinjiang is an autonomous region in the west of China and has a sister relationship with the city of Shanghai to carry out the task of poverty alleviation as ordered by the central government. VET02 school is responsible for supporting the vocational school in Kashgar, Xinjiang. In March 2016, a working group, led by the school headmaster, visited the vocational school in Kashgar to conduct research. The group undertook a field trip to the training base, listened to a presentation about the status of vocational teachers, the curriculum framework and the needs of the school. An investigation of the local economic development enabled VET02 to propose a specific assistance plan for the e-commerce profession. The plan was based on the actual situation of the two schools and aimed to facilitate local economic development. The plan consisted of three aspects: (1) construction of training bases, including e-commerce warehousing and a distribution experiment training room, and express delivery (transportation) experiment training room; (2) development of logistics information technology education, covering digital resource application, e-commerce logistics resources, cloud platform application and curriculum development and design; (3) provision of teacher training to improve the quality of teachers in the partner school.

The action plan was finalised on the basis of this preliminary investigation and the return visit by delegations of the vocational school in Xinjiang. After nearly a week of in-depth discussions, the two schools reached agreement on the areas of intensive training, professional teaching standards, training centre construction, special skills teaching and training room construction. The two partner schools combined ideas and planned to build a demonstration major in e-commerce. During the discussions, it was agreed that VET02 would send teachers to its partner school for discipline construction and demonstration teaching, and the partner school selected leaders and teachers to visit VET02 for training.

Many VET schools have not only engaged in sharing experiences with other schools domestically, but have also developed partnerships to support schools in other countries by sharing their experiences. For example, 20 vocational school teachers and teacher trainers from Laos took part in two parallel pilot training courses conducted by Chinese professionals in the local vocational training centre in Pingdu in August 2018. The vocational training sector in Laos faces challenges in keeping pace with economic and social developments, providing impetus for value creation and further promoting regional market integration. China faced the same challenges a few years ago and Pingdu is a good location to share its development experience of agribusiness with the counterparts from Laos. VET07 played a key role by sharing its vocational education experience of developing agribusiness with the support of its German partners. This example demonstrates a unique international cooperation within a trilateral partnership for vocational education development internationally.

Reforming school management system

Today, vocational schools face many more internal and external changes and challenges than in the past. They are required to deal with multiple stakeholders such as students and their parents, teachers, enterprises and governments, become involved in a number of activities such as forecasting the needs of the labour market, organising teaching and training, student management (e.g. dining hall and accommodation), teaching resources management (e.g. consumption of raw materials, training machines and training base), and teachers' performance evaluation. With the introduction of new technology and new managerial practices, the school management system is evolving and reforming.

Given its strength in new technology, VET02 has made full use of IT and has developed an intelligent school management system named 'one campus'. The 'one campus' concept consists of so-called '5 systems +3 models' where 'five systems' refers to the student administration system, curriculum management system, human resource management system, finance management system and capital management system, and 'three models' includes the teaching management model, administration management model and service management model. The student administration system, for instance, establishes a life cycle management system for students, driven by big data. The system collects student data and forms a student portrait with an algorithm model (see Figure 5.4). The curriculum management system introduces external big data sources, such as the Baidu search index to track the popularity of existing and potential professionals, enabling the school's curriculum framework to closely follow industry needs. The curriculum management system also introduces an intelligence monitoring system to collect information on vocational education and the employment market. It helps the school management quickly grasp key information and understand the overall situation (see Figure 5.5 for an illustration). With regard to human resources management, finance management and capital management, the curriculum combines the 'Internet of Things', mobile Internet and big data to achieve the most economical configuration of resources. Collecting all data and results, the 'one campus' system can generate a visualised report to school management for decision-making.

Figure 5.4 The algorithm model.
Source: Data collected in 2018.

Each system or model follows an '8-shape spiral' management process (see Figure 5.6). The upper part of the 8-shape spiral is built for real-time operation monitoring, providing a powerful early warning function. The user can view the real-time status after logging into the system platform. The lower part of the 8-shape spiral is built to generate a diagnosis report. The diagnosis report consists of four parts. The first part provides an overview of the self-diagnosis including the main problems, improvement measures and improvement effects. The second part shows 'unfulfilled indicators' highlighting the indicator data that is not up to the standard. The third part consists of an 'early warning information record form', which reports whether goals are met in real-time monitoring. The fourth part provides a 'self-diagnosis table', showing all monitored diagnosis data.

VET03 is located in the same city as VET02 (i.e. Shanghai); its management system is built with the support of Japanese enterprises. Under the strong

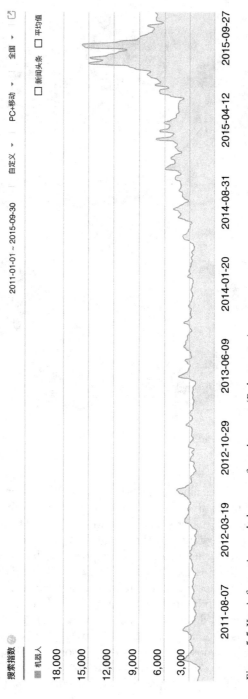

Figure 5.5 Key information and changes of employment (Robot sector).
Source: School 'one campus' system.

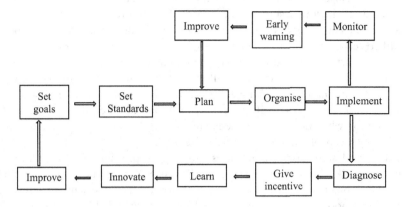

Figure 5.6 The '8-shape spiral' model.
Source: Data collected in 2018.

influence of Japanese corporate culture, the system focuses on a different aspect of management, namely discretion and intelligence. Everything is digitalised and documented. Authorised staff can check the detailed working status of every equipment, such as which unit is working, what procedure the unit is working on, who is operating the unit as well as detailed information on the operator. The system also keeps track of what materials have been used and how many materials have been used by each student or operator. The efficiency of VET03 has been largely improved with the introduction of the new technology and diagnosis system.

Teachers' development

A strong vocational education is inseparably linked to high-quality vocational education teachers. Unlike general education, vocational teaching should place equal emphasis on theory and practical skills in order to serve industry needs and meet labour market demand.

Currently, most vocational teachers are recruited from universities and most of them do not have much practical experience. Government and schools have been concerned about ensuring teachers have both theoretical and practical skills (so-called 'dual certificate' teachers) and have made great efforts and explored avenues to develop capable teachers. The common practice shared by selected schools (e.g. VET02, VET05 and VET06) is to dispatch teachers to work in enterprises on a regular basis. Through on-the-job training or appointments in the enterprises, teachers can learn about production processes and be familiar with the specific content of the relevant positions (or types of work), operating standards, employment standards and management systems. In addition, schools actively introduce technical experts and masters from enterprises as part-time teachers, and cooperate with school teachers to carry out professional and curriculum development, and classroom teaching.

Working closely with enterprises, schools (e.g. VET04 and VET06) have developed a curriculum system and standards designed to improve the quality of teachers, thus not only ensuring that teachers in schools become 'dual certificate' qualified teachers, but also opening the door to experts in enterprises who wish to teach in schools. Based on the core competences required by HRD policies and workplace demands, the curriculum system is mainly composed of three aspects: teacher literacy, teaching ability and professional ability. Teacher literacy refers to teachers' theoretical knowledge and morality. Teachers influence students not only by imparting knowledge but also by being good role models; they need to be a capable teacher with correct moral codes. Teaching ability includes curriculum design, teaching methods, language expression and IT application. Professional skills refer to professional technical skills in terms of the latest technical developments and relevant industry information. The teaching itself is also shared by schools and enterprises as teaching literacy and ability courses are led by the school, while the professional ability courses are led by enterprises.

In addition to the above practices to develop teachers, providing continuous assistance and a platform is vital to the development of teachers. VET01 emphasises the fostering of young generation teachers. When a new teacher is recruited, the school assigns two mentors; one is in charge of training in administration issues and student supervision, and the other focuses on enhancing teaching skills. In addition, the vocational teachers are responsible for taking care of students' daily lives as most students stay in the school's dormitory. After students graduate, teachers are required to follow up and collect information about graduates' most recent status. These tasks place high demands on teachers' abilities and skills in student administration. In terms of teaching skills, the school selects and sends new teachers to training seminars held by the Municipal Commission and Ministry of Education. The school sends a few high performers abroad for further training at the school's overseas partner institutions and then promotes them as leaders when they return. With this continuous assistance from the school, these young generation teachers adapt quickly to the school's environment.

Enhancing students' learning experience and career development

One important task of VET schools is to enhance students' learning experiences which potentially lead to better teaching and training outcomes. Students' potential career development also attracts the attention of policymakers, educators, enterprises and students. There are a number of issues related to enhancing students' learning experience; the following sections provide a detailed elaboration.

Revising teaching materials

Vocational schools normally use national planning textbooks, except in foundation courses. Schools have the autonomy to use provincially approved textbooks

or the schools' self-edited materials, which is a common practice across all selected schools. For instance, the teaching materials used in VET01 include three
categories strictly in accordance with the requirements of the Beijing Municipal
Education Authority. The foundation courses use the national planning textbooks from the Higher Education Press or the People's Education Publishing
House; the professional core courses use the Beijing curriculum reform textbooks; the school-based courses use a textbook edited by the school itself. The
development of self-edited textbook reflects the characteristics of each school.

In VET01, the school-based courses and curriculum were designed by the
school and were intended to satisfy the individual development of learners,
adapting to professional needs and serving lifelong learning. This approach can
be summarised in the expression 'one body, two wings and three services'. The
'one body' refers to the 'one' school-based curriculum developed for vocational
education as the main body. The 'one body' curriculum consists of 34 courses
with the three major categories of humanities and arts, physical and mental
health, and professional development. The 'two wings' refer to social training
courses and primary and secondary school experience courses provided by the
school. The 'two wings' courses are derived from the 'one body'. The social
training courses 'wing' consists of 39 modules, such as improving quality of life,
historic and cultural heritage of Beijing, and workplace practices. The primary
and secondary school experience courses 'wing' consists of 29 modules focusing on professional experience and historic and cultural heritage of Beijing. The
'three services' refers to 'one body two wings' courses for secondary vocational
education students, students in primary and lower secondary schools in terms
of occupational experience, and citizens, enterprises and community in terms of
continuing education. The process of establishing this kind of system involves
drafting a school-based syllabus, building a training base or classroom, preparing course handouts, and editing and publishing school-based textbook. In addition, with the introduction of advanced IT and cloud-based technology, the
school-based textbook is digitalised into an electronic textbook for small private
online courses (SPOC) and/or massive open online courses (MOOC) to serve
the community better.

Reforming teaching and training methods

In an era of new technology, teaching methods have been developed to meet
new requirements such as interactive teaching and cost-efficiency. Students
are required to show distinctive skills such as Internet thinking, creativity and
open-mindedness.

Taking machining training as example, machining is a material-removal process in which a piece of raw material is cut into a desired final shape and size.
After removing some of the raw material, the remaining part (i.e. machined
component) can interact with other components as designed. It is a fundamental
process widely used in the manufacturing industry. In the past, non-computer-
aided machining required manual control with step-by-step action. With modern

computer numerical control, the manufacturing process is highly automated. Instructions are delivered to the machine in the form of a graphic computer-aided design file, then transformed into specific commands and executed. In order to learn machining, students thus need to know the underpinning theories, the coding (with computer-aided design software and commands) and the execution on the machine. Since the production of components might require the use of a number of different tools, modern machines often combine multiple tools into a single 'cell' (i.e. the machine), placing high demands on skills in terms of increased comprehension and complexity.

In VET05 the machining programmes offered are the school's historic strength. Traditionally, the teaching of machining consisted of three classroom-delivered courses based on the machining process, including theory, coding in the computer lab and practice on the machine. These courses were arranged in sequential order. For instance, the first semester covered theory, followed by coding in the second semester and then four weeks of practice. This method led to disjointed learning so that when students started to code on computer or on the machine, most could not recall what they had been taught in the theory class. Therefore, the school integrated the three courses into one course and increased the four weeks of practice to seven weeks (see Figure 5.7). The new course uses the teaching materials prepared by the teaching staff. Furthermore, for the sake of integration, the school moved the classroom into the computer lab and set up a small computer lab next to the training base for machining. The revised course therefore consists of a first session (i.e. 30–45 mins.) for theory, immediately followed by coding on computer under the guidance of theory teachers and practices instructors. The computers in the lab are installed with software which simulates the authentic interface on the machine. Students can execute their commands and correct accordingly. After adjustment or correction, and when the simulated results are correct, students proceed to the training base to process the raw materials.

In contrast to the traditional disjointed teaching and practices, the current teaching model shortens the gap between learning, reflection and practice. Students can put the theory they have just learnt into practice. The machining process requires various types of tools such as blades and drill saws. In order to remove volume from the raw materials, the tools spin at incredibly high speed. Fatal injuries to the controllers (i.e. students or teachers) can result if the commands executed are incorrect. Simulation software can minimise the risk. In addition, the high-accuracy machines are expensive (1,000,000 yuan each or above); repeatedly executed incorrect commands will shorten its service life.

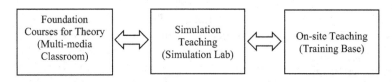

Figure 5.7 Theory-practice integration in VET05.

The raw materials for machining (i.e. steel in most cases) are costly. China's secondary vocational schools are not allowed to collect tuition fees from students, making it necessary for schools to raise money to cover the cost incurred during teaching. If schools use fibre as a cheap substitute for steel, the working experience for students is totally different. The introduction of simulation software significantly reduces the consumption of raw materials without compromising teaching outcomes.

Being a supplementary to the 'integrated' teaching model, the school creates a teaching-productive exercise model. The school works with certain small- and medium-sized factories which cannot afford to purchase the necessary equipment. The factories send the semi-finished products to the schools to get these products fine finishing by teachers in the school. For the school, this means that full use is made of its investment in the equipment, and for the teachers who do not have much experience with machining, this is a good opportunity to learn. As part of the agreement between school and factory, students can observe the production process or participate during the early stages of production. The advantage for the factories is that they do not have to buy machining equipment. This model is thus beneficial to all stakeholders.

In addition, other efforts have been made to reform training methods. For example, VET01 has reformed its midterm examination method. The examinations for foundations courses (e.g. literature and mathematics) and professional courses have been changed from closed book to open book examination. Taking the mathematics examination as example, a 'Mathematician Story' project was added in the examination as a way of assessing knowledge. Students are required to prepare a handwritten poster and are allowed to customise the topic and content within the scope of the knowledge they have learnt. The professional courses examinations also adopt a variety of flexible assessment methods. Students are organised by teachers to conduct on-the-spot investigations, actual operations, data collection and analysis, and practical report presentations. These aforementioned changes highlight vocational students' autonomy and creative learning ability rather than simply memorising information.

VET01 introduced an effective interactive classroom teaching project in 2012 in which students' interest in learning resources and knowledge is encouraged through the use of electronic devices. The smart interactive classrooms use tablets, PCs and wireless networks to achieve leap-forward teaching innovation in all aspects of pre-class, in-class and after-class activities. The teacher prepares the resource library in advance on the server to integrate the lesson plans, slides, exercises, pictures and audio/video materials, and shares these via electronic tablets. This method enhances interaction not only between students and teachers, but also between various knowledge bands among students. Students can follow the teacher's lecture, participate in interactive demonstrations and undertake exercise tests in real time through the devices. With real-time feedback, teachers can see the test results, how well the students understand the learning points of the course, and then conduct more targeted explanations based on the test results.

The introduction of the intelligent interactive classroom establishes teachers as the service providers, leaders, organisers, encouragers and collaborators of the student learning process. The traditional mode centred on the teaching itself has become a teaching mode based on student's learning. Students can be better motivated by transitioning from passive learning to active learning. In addition, traditional classroom teaching with a low level of interaction has caused individual students to lose interest in learning, whereas self-investigation, collaborative research and group study largely liberate students' thinking and activity space, stimulating students' interest in learning and participating in discussions.

VET01 also equips training rooms with multimedia facilities, closely combined with different professional training environments. For example, the school has built a semicircular screen in the comprehensive training classroom and uses three projectors to create a virtual environment such as Tiananmen Square, the Forbidden City and other attractions for students to practice tour guide skills. In tea art classes, teachers first perform tea brewing demonstrations, but due to the limited operating space, the students in the back rows cannot see the teacher's operation method. Teachers therefore connect a camera to the interactive whiteboard or LCD screen, so that students can observe and learn, thus enhancing efficiency of teaching and learning.

In order to ensure that the electronic devices can better serve education, the school information centre deploys a special team dedicated to the functioning of tablets, which not only ensures the normal operation of the teaching via tablets, but also provides technical support for the next stage of reform. With proper guidance and appropriate intervention, a more relaxed and interesting learning environment can be created for the students and their learning experience to be enhanced.

Fostering of professionalism

The fostering of professionalism has become one of the key focus areas in China's VET, while being a good citizen has been embedded in Chinese culture. In addition to being good citizens, students are encouraged to be skilled workers with soft skills such as communication skills as well as being patient and having moral virtues. At the same time, students are trained to achieve perfection and professionalism.

An example of this approach has been seen in VET01 since its establishment. The school has taken upon itself the important mission of providing services for major political events in Beijing for which fostering professionalism is vital in relation to all students and teachers. In 2017, the school created a progressive moral education model referred to as the 'one main line, two footholds and three stages of progress'. This model adopts socialist core values as a main line, relies on two footholds (skills needed at work and sustainable student development) and progresses through three stages. The first stage focuses on ensuring first year students develop a good personal image. Students need to be immersed in a strongly etiquette-oriented environment and atmosphere in school, learning etiquette from a textbook. This stage lays the foundation for the next one. In the second stage, students are encouraged to apply etiquette and communication skills in daily life. Students are required to participate in etiquette competitions as a team and test the outcomes of their learning. During the third stage, students are assigned to undertake service works as practices at various events. This model helps students practise and develop an outstanding sense of professionalism and moral sentiment during practice sessions. In addition, 14 moral education activities were designed and implemented in 2017. Each activity has a theme, a plan, an evaluation, a summary and feedback, which complete the loop. In all activities, the students' participation rate reached 98% in 2017, and that was much higher than previous years. Participating in important political tasks or important foreign affairs services is an indispensable part of the school's moral education since it closely links school education with a variety of social and political activities which, in turn, promote a high level of student political responsibility.

VET06 presents a different example of ethic and professional education, as can be seen in the 'Students' Daily Behavioural Standards Study Manual' the school implemented as a compulsory course for all students. The manual covers three main aspects, namely moral quality, professional ability and self-development ability. In addition to the manual, the 'three self-education' (self-discipline, self-awareness and autonomy), 'peer counselling' and so on ensure that all students develop moral character and related behaviour. Similarly, VET03 has developed a special project focusing on professionalism and practical application. The project is progressive, graded from easy to difficult, and provides for a series of themed activities such as 'cultivating the heart with craft', 'refining craft with the heart' and 'shaping the soul with craft'. All of these activities were developed for the purpose of improving the self-cognitive ability and social cognitive ability of students.

Entrepreneurship in vocational education

With the rapid development of the national economy, there have been ongoing changes in industrial structures. It is widely recognised that VET largely facilitates students' transition from school to the workplace. Besides cultivating the skilled workforce needed in the labour markets and in enterprises, entrepreneurship and entrepreneurship education have emerged as a key theme in China's VET (Ministry of Education, 2018). For example, in 2009, VET04 started to explore how to promote students' entrepreneurship and encourage them to choose their careers freely or start their own businesses.

Entrepreneurship is a complicated and creative undertaking. In order to achieve success, entrepreneurs must not only have strong entrepreneurial awareness and entrepreneurial motivation, but also strong entrepreneurial practice with accumulated experience. The initiative of young students to start a business is often inextricably linked with their entrepreneurial ability. Therefore, VET04's entrepreneurship programme is developed on the basis of students' entrepreneurial tendencies.

During the preparation stage of taking entrepreneurship programme, the school prepared school-based textbooks suitable for students' employment and entrepreneurship based on the status of local economic development. The textbook entitled 'Employment and Entrepreneurship Guides' is offered to students in Year 3. The book includes classroom teaching on entrepreneurial knowledge and the cultivation of entrepreneurial concepts, so that the students can understand the concept of entrepreneurship, starting a business and building a career. The school invites successful entrepreneurs to give lectures and interact with students; it organises entrepreneurial simulation activities and holds annual entrepreneurial design and career planning competitions to develop students' entrepreneurial skills. The school also organises 'Start Your Business' training with the Department of Human Resources and Social Security Training Centre to assist students in understanding the basic skills of management and learning to write business plans in order to improve students' entrepreneurial abilities. In addition, the school provides support to promising projects and good entrepreneurs from the previous stage, and conducts substantive entrepreneurial practice sessions. Peer counselling and tracking services further help students solve practical problems encountered in the process of learning about entrepreneurship. In order to ensure the quality of guidance provided, the school establishes an entrepreneurial mentor appointment system and builds a complete team of entrepreneurial teachers. The team is comprised of teachers and entrepreneurs who have experience in entrepreneurship education, as well as public officials from economic management departments. These people are responsible for organising various training courses and practical activities to help students solve technical difficulties and to guide students through the process of entrepreneurial activities. In addition, the school also establishes a venture capital fund to provide appropriate financial support to students' entrepreneurship education. By working together with student associations to set up special entrepreneurial associations, the school encourages students to participate in entrepreneurial activities based on their own professional knowledge and skills to start a new business. With the implementation of relevant management systems, evaluation systems and incentive policies, the school has created an environment for students to start their business.

Up to the present, 12 students have become small business operators running campus-based start-ups. Over 200 students have participated in the school's entrepreneurial programme. For example, the vehicle maintenance centre is founded and operated by ten students who have worked in the automobile repair and maintenance area for over one year. This workshop has become the first choice for school bus repairs and maintenance and for cleaning and maintenance of over 300 school teachers' private cars. The electronics appliances maintenance centre is planned to provide installation and maintenance service to electrical equipment such as computer, mobiles and earphones. Jingxin Laundry provides laundry and self-service laundry services to nearly 5,000 students in the school and undertakes cleaning of private trains and school bus seat covers.

The school has also set up a Cultural Park to serve the cultural construction of the campus through student start-ups. Students are encouraged to plan and design various activities, create a campus culture atmosphere, enhance their own cultural literacy, create a school-specific brand, and learn to operate a business. For example, participation in the riddle competition is a characteristic of the school. Every year, the school sends a team to participate in this competition in Singapore. By encouraging the creation of themed riddles and planning of cultural activities, the school is able to improve the overall quality of students and promotes the construction of a campus culture. The school has set up a science and technology park to support innovative projects and act as an incubator. The building area measures 10,000 square metres and the total investment is 30 million yuan. The facility has various training and entrepreneurial facilities covering major study areas, including automotive, economics, trade, IT, numerical control, electrical engineering and human resources development. Multifunctional halls, lecture halls, business centre with conference rooms, training rooms and other public service facilities are also available. This project aims to encourage and attract outstanding scientific and technological talent inside and outside the school, and provide support for the school's entrepreneurial programme, entrepreneurial practice and potential start-up investors.

Career planning and development

With regard to students' professional life, career planning and future development, a number of initiatives have been introduced using different models. Currently, career planning is taught separately in vocational schools as a series of compulsory courses. In 2008, the Ministry of Education stipulated that these courses had to be offered to vocational students from 2009 (Ministry of Education, 2008b). During the first semester of Year 1, the course covers career planning (a total 32–36 teaching hours), followed by the second semester of Year 1 focusing on professional ethics and law (32–36 teaching hours). The first semester of Year 2 covers political economy and society (32–36 teaching hours) and the second semester of Year 2 covers philosophy and life (32–36 teaching hours). The Department of Education requires that all vocational schools use the textbooks edited by the Department itself.

Given the relatively low autonomy of schools in offering these courses, we have used the data collected at VET06 to illustrate the current status of implementation of the career planning courses. Our survey was distributed to employers (e.g. managers or administrative supervisors of automobile 4S shop, maintenance factory and dealers) and students and teachers, covering various aspects of the career planning course (e.g. importance of the course, content of the textbook, teaching methods and feedback from employers).

The first finding is that all managers, teachers and students believed that offering of career planning courses is important. The courses guide students to establish correct professional concepts and professional ideals, learn to conduct career planning according to social needs and characteristics, and regulate and adjust their actions, all of which are important to create conditions for a smooth employment and entrepreneurship after graduation. Among the business managers,

92% believed that it is important for secondary vocational students to build a growth ladder in their professional lives, undertake career planning and future development. The managers indicated that it is helpful for students to know the path towards career growth, to plan for future development and to adjust their mentality so as not to rush for a job offer. All managers who responded to our survey believed that for the future development of secondary vocational students, career planning needed to be evaluated and adjusted timeously; 73% believed that secondary vocational students need to adjust their professional lives and career development goals. All the teachers who responded to our survey believed that career planning is important for students' career development, and 76.19% thought this to be extremely important. With regard to the students, 42% recognised the importance of the courses, but only 26% of students considered the courses to be extremely important. It can be seen that students do not attach great importance to these courses; they believe that only skill-related professional courses are important, and the philosophical, cultural and moral foundation courses are of comparatively less significance.

The current textbooks and supporting materials are written by the Ministry of Education in accordance with the requirements of the syllabus of moral education curriculum in secondary vocational schools (Ministry of Education, 2008a). In terms of frequency of use of the current textbook content and materials, both students and teachers did not appear to frequently use these resources – the vast majority is only used during class, with a high indication that the resources are only occasionally or never used. It is clear that the teaching materials are used to complete a task in class, but they do not help to extend the students in real-life settings. In terms of satisfaction with textbooks and materials layout, students and teachers do not appear to be satisfied with the current textbook as well as supportive learning materials. The textbook only contains case studies, links and other text materials, which are considered monotonous by the students. The textbooks and learning materials are not attractive to students, lacking clear task guidelines and answers to questions. The student survey figures show that 42% of the students were neither satisfied nor dissatisfied, and 12% of the students were dissatisfied with the course materials. Only 42% of the students indicated that they were very satisfied. The teacher survey indicates that only 9.52% of the teachers expressed their satisfaction, and 80.95% of the teachers felt neutral about the teaching materials. In terms of the alignment between teaching materials and students' majors, the teachers believed that the level of alignment between current teaching materials and students' majors is very low. However, the students expressed the opinion that the alignment of teaching materials and majors is high. The reason for this contrasting response is that most of the teachers have adjusted their teaching materials to suit the students' majors. In terms of how well the current teaching materials assist the students, both students and teachers believed that the materials used in the current textbooks are average in assisting students' learning. Responses indicate that 3.09% of the students thought that the materials were extremely ineffective, 8.25% of the students thought that they were ineffective, 52% thought that their effectiveness was average, and only

37% believed them to be very effective. The teacher questionnaire indicated that 15% of teachers believed that the materials were ineffective and 75% of teachers believed that their effectiveness was average.

With regard to the issue of how to organise teaching, students and teachers showed different preferences. Classroom teaching was favoured by 50.5% of the students, while this mode was favoured by only 31.82% of the teachers. Group teaching was welcomed by 59.09% of the teachers, but only by 17.5% of the students. The differences in responses are caused by the fact that teachers want to involve students through group teaching, but students do not like to participate in group learning. Students like classroom teaching where teachers talk in front of a blackboard and the students simply listen.

In terms of methods used to present knowledge during teaching, the most common include teacher's oral presentation, video, case analysis, role play and presentation of text materials and pictures. The survey results show that teachers were very fond of using video, case studies, role plays and pictures, while oral presentations and text materials were not popular. Students also liked the above-mentioned knowledge presentation methods, especially case analyses, followed by videos. The least welcome method among students was role play, while teachers liked to use role play the most.

With regard to classroom question-and-answer activities, teachers liked to use students' active answers and group competitions to obtain answers to questions; 37.5% of the teachers liked the students to answer the questions proactively and 37.5% of the teachers preferred the student group competition. Students preferred to answer proactively, rather than being selected to answer, or favoured group competitions.

With regard to the degree of enthusiasm for participation in classroom activities, both students and teachers thought the level of participation in the classroom activities to be rather low. Responses indicated that 28% of the teachers believed that students knew the answer but did not participate, and 28% of the teachers believed that students did not know the answer and waited for the others in the classroom to participate. When teachers conducted classroom activities, the proportion of students who did not participate in the activity was indicated to be 53.85%; of these, 39.56% of the students knew the answer but did not want to participate, 10.99% of the students did not know the answer and did not want to participate, 3.3% of the students felt that the class had nothing to do with them. Therefore, in the classroom, it appears to be common that students are not involved in classroom activities, but are rather passive recipients of what is being taught.

The survey results regarding student control behaviour in the classroom indicated consistency between the teachers and the students: 73% of teachers and 90.33% of students believed that students could control their behaviour in the classroom and learn from the teachers. Among the students, 41.94% indicated that they could control their behaviour well and 48.39% could generally control their behaviour. When participating in classroom activities, 91.01% of the students were able to follow the teacher's instruction, but 43.82% of the students could not comprehend what was taught. It can be seen that the students have not mastered the ethic knowledge learnt in the classroom, and hence, the effectiveness of classroom activities is low. However, most of the students could control their behaviour, but the enthusiasm of independent thinking was low. Students were able to refrain from talking, falling asleep and playing on their mobile phones. In addition, 81.82% of the teachers and 56.98% of the students believed that students only listened to the lectures but did not take notes during class. Results regarding the classroom learning process indicated that the proportion of active thinkers was 42.71%, and the proportion of occasionally active thinkers was 52.08%.

In addition to the school's efforts to develop courses which address students' careers, employers' feedback is also critical to the development of career planning courses and contributes to fulfilling employers' obligations in supporting the development of VET.

In the corporate questionnaire, 50% of the managers indicated that they believed that the career planning awareness of interns from the school was at an average level, and 29% thought that career planning awareness among these interns was above average, while 21% believed that it was low. In terms of setting career planning objectives, 78% believed that the career goals of the interns were somewhat clear, and only 21% believed that the career goals of the interns were very clear. In comparison, 61.9% of the teachers believed that the career goals of the students in their class were somewhat clear. Only 23.81% of the teachers believed that the students' career goals were very clear. With regard to whether the interns from VET06 could align their own situations with their career planning, 93% of the managers and 60% of the teachers thought they could, while 7% of the managers and 40% of the teachers thought they could not. On the question of whether school interns could design career planning in conjunction with the trends of the industry, 100% of managers and 61.90% of teachers believed that they could, and 38.1% of the teachers thought they could not.

Overall, the importance of career planning is fully recognised by policymakers, educators, students and enterprises. Career planning courses enhance students' career awareness, ability to set career objectives and ability to align their own situations with their career planning. However, greater efforts are still needed in order to address students' level of awareness regarding their professional lives, career planning and future development.

Conclusion

In this chapter, we have continued our case studies by focusing on a number of important issues, such as ongoing curriculum development, strategic transition, reforming school management system, teachers' development and enhancing students' learning experiences and career development. These case studies have demonstrated that the scale of China's VET has been expanding rapidly, undertaking more tasks than ever before, such as providing training to community residents and public, training teachers from less-developed areas and helping disadvantaged groups. China's VET is also evolving and upgrading. With the introduction of new technology, smart and intelligent management systems have been developed. New technology is also widely applied during teaching and training to enhance the level of interaction between teachers and students. The significance of vocational schools to students is not limited to obtaining skills for a job; rather, they have become a place for students to learn to be good citizens and to learn to plan their professional lives and future career development. Despite many reforms and achievements, certain issues still need to be addressed. Furthermore, with China's deepening economic and industrial reforms, there are further changes and challenges confronting the VET system. The following chapter will discuss the future development of China's VET and will offer some constructive suggestions.

References

China Daily, 2014. Chongqing invested 1.2 trillion yuan in infrastructure and promulgated the implementation of national 'One belt and One Road' Strategy and the 'Yangtze River Economic Belt' [online] http://cn.chinadaily.com.cn Available at http://www.chinadaily.com.cn/dfpd/cq/2014-12/19/content_19125406.htm [accessed on 19 February 2019]

China Daily, 2018. Increased consumption and rapid growth power e-commerce [online] http://www.chinadaily.com.cn Available at http://www.chinadaily.com.cn/a/201811/21/WS5bf4c510a310eff30328a17c.html [accessed on 10 February 2019]

Ministry of Education, 2008a. Notice of the Ministry of Education on printing and distributing the syllabus for moral education courses in secondary vocational schools [online] http://www.moe.gov.cn Available at http://www.moe.gov.cn/srcsite/A07/moe_950/200812/t20081210_79005.html [accessed on 16 February 2019]

Ministry of Education, 2008b. Opinions of the Ministry of Education on the curriculum setting and teaching arrangement of moral education in secondary vocational schools [online] http://www.moe.gov.cn Available at http://www.moe.gov.cn/srcsite/A07/moe_950/200812/t20081210_79006.html [accessed on 11 February 2019]

Ministry of Education, 2018. Vocational education ushers in the golden period [online] http://www.moe.gov.cn Available at http://www.moe.gov.cn/jyb_xwfb/moe_2082/zl_2018n/2018_zl16/201802/t20180227_327950.html [accessed on 17 February 2019]

Xinhua, 2017. Fujian opened the first subway line to enter the subway era [online] http://www.news.cn Available at http://www.xinhuanet.com/local/2017-01/06/c_1120260653.htm [accessed on 9 January 2019]

6 Ongoing challenges and future development of China's VET system

This book has presented a holistic view of China's VET system. The efforts made jointly by policymakers, vocational education school employees and enterprises have led to tremendous achievements by China's vocational education through reform and development. At the same time, VET still faces many challenges. In terms of future development, China is set to become a developed society in all social and economic areas. To this end, the country will take a new pathway towards the economy of the future through further urbanisation and the promotion of a high quality of life for all its citizens. In terms of improving the quality of human capital, further efforts will be made to develop vocational education, which, no doubt, will lead to new opportunities for developing an advanced VET system. In this final chapter, we focus on a number of meaningful issues and related implications, including the role of government and reform of the VET system within the context of the unique characteristics of a transitional economy, as well as the directions for future development.

The role of government

Since the 21st century, with the increasing emphasis on the development of VET by the state and society, the development of China's VET has leapt in both scale and quality. The comprehensive strength of VET has gradually improved and international influence has continuously increased. A high-quality technical and skilled workforce provides greatly demanded human capital to support economic and social development in China.

Chinese governments and their educational agencies play critical roles in shaping China's VET and governing system. Under the leadership of the central government, the Ministry of Education has the authority to implement national policy for vocational education to achieve the goal of modernisation and to improve national competition. Provincial education administrations are given instructions by the central government regarding how to manage the educational institutes in their provinces. Vocational schools must request approval from the corresponding government administrations on a number of issues such as setting up new majors, recruiting teachers, and spending funding appropriately. However, the functioning of the governing system has not been totally smooth and is still seriously plagued by segmentation. The relationship between the central government and local governments is rather vague, though legally, the division of administrative authority with regard to VET between the central government and local governments is relatively clear according to the law. Article 11 of the Vocational Educational Law of the People's Republic of China stipulates:

> The administrative department of education under the State Council shall be responsible for the overall planning, comprehensive coordination and macro management of vocational education.... The local governments at or above the county level shall strengthen the leadership, coordination and supervision of their vocational education within their respective administrative regions.
>
> (The National People's Congress of the
> People's Republic China, 1996)

This clearly gives administrative authority and power to local governments. However, a closer look reveals that the central government is actually in charge. In addition, the relationship between the education departments and other departments is rather vague. At present, China's vocational education system adopts a multilevel management system involving governments, departments, industries and enterprises. The divisions of management are separate, with overlapping capacities, influencing the optimal allocation of vocational education resources and affecting the normal functioning of government agencies at different levels.

An inter-ministerial joint conference system for VET has been established under the leadership of the State Council in recent years in order to manage the relationships and responsibilities among the various areas of management. This inter-ministerial joint conference system is not new, but in comparison with the previous 'version', the current version has been changed by using a leader who is in charge of education within the State Council to replace the former one with a leader from the Minister of Education as the convener. In addition, two deputy conveners are assigned to the leader of the Ministry of Education and the Deputy Secretary-General of the State Council who assists in the education work (State Council, 2019). This situation highlights the importance attached to VET by the State Council, as well as the power of the joint conference system in the reform of vocational education. With this enhanced power, the functions of the joint ministries conference system are largely expanded, to coordinate and supervise the implementation of the major decisions made by the Party Central Committee and the State Council on VET, coordinate national VET, and solve major problems in VET. Major reforms and innovation in VET have been planned, following the suggestions provided by the National Vocational Education Guidance Advisory Committee. Furthermore, the joint ministries have been increased from six to nine departments, namely the Ministry of Education, the National Development and Reform Commission, the Ministry of Industry and Information Technology, the Ministry of Finance, the Ministry of Human

Resources and Social Security, the Ministry of Agriculture and Rural Affairs, the State-owned Assets Supervision and Administration Commission, the State Administration of Taxation, and the Poverty Alleviation Office (State Council, 2019). The aim of adding three departments, namely the State-owned Assets Supervision and Administration Commission, the State Administration of Taxation, and the Ministry of Industry and Information Technology, is to break the barriers for more integration between the government agencies, VET, industry sectors and enterprises, particularly small- and medium-sized businesses.

Local governments are required to effectively guarantee the healthy development of VET. In accordance with the actual development of VET in different regions, local governments first accelerate the process by promoting the development of local education laws and regulations based on the relevant national law and regulations. Local governments also formulate the corresponding implementation methods. By applying multiple means to coordinate the interests of all stakeholders, local governments are responsible for building a close departmental cooperation to promote engagement between VET, industry sectors and enterprises. In addition, a third-party independent VET monitoring and supervision system overseeing the performance of local VET has been adopted by the local governments.

In general, in order to develop China's VET, the emphasis has shifted from bureaucratic administration to effectively implementing the relevant policies and regulations as well as monitoring and supervising VET's performance with the introduction of ongoing reforms.

Reforming the VET system with unique patterns

Emergence of the VET system

The development of China's vocational system has undergone a continuous reform process. Originally, it was labelled a 'decapitated' education system (*du-antou jiaoyu*) which ended at the upper secondary vocational level. With the introduction of the '3+2' and '3+4' models and the independent enrolment scheme in universities, the opportunities for vocational graduates to receive higher education increased. The upper secondary vocational level evolved into a VET system with higher levels of continuity, seen to be parallel to general academic education. Although the channels between each educational stage were not wide and the connections between lower and higher levels of education were not effective enough, the VET system initially emerged with both vertical and horizontal expansion (see Figure 6.1).

From a basic framework to a modern system with Chinese characteristics, China's VET and VET system have undergone a great change with their own development path. The years 1985, 2005 and 2014 are milestones in the formation and development of the VET system. In 1985, a blueprint for the construction of the system was proposed in order to establish a VET system from primary to advanced level with industry support, a better structure and the ability to connect with general education. During the next 30 years, the system basically operated

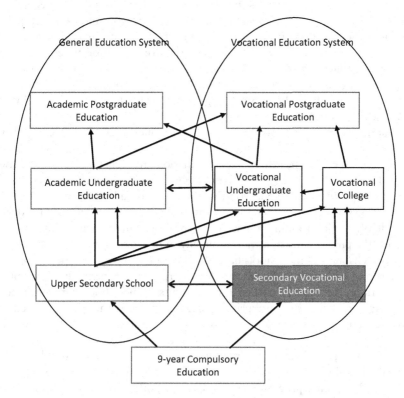

Figure 6.1 General education system and vocational education system.

according to this blueprint. From 2005, Chinese characteristics and modern attributes were emphasised and proposed with the purpose of integrating the VET system with the socialist market economic system, meeting the needs of the people for lifelong learning, and achieving close alignment with labour market demand. In 2014, a development plan for the VET system was more comprehensively and concretely proposed. This proposal transformed VET from an isolated 'single level' to a 'category' which linked with the general education system at multiple levels (State Council, 2014a). The plan further reinforced VET's function as the essence of education with the consideration of lifelong learning and career development of citizens.

Providing general training for public citizens

Continuous development of the economy and society results in people having a variety of needs for training, and vocational schools can provide the relevant training programmes to meet the needs of the labour market as well as the demographic changes in China. For example, continuous economic development increases the frequency of job changes, requiring vocational schools to provide vocational training to meet the needs of people changing jobs in their related industry. In the past, vocational skills training of citizens and various types of re-employment training in society were important supplements to academic education, but most vocational schools were perceived as minor players since they focused on educating vocational students. Today, the importance of vocational skills training has emerged and vocational schools are required to expand their function to provide skills training programmes to public citizens beyond vocational school students.

In addition, the school-aged population continues to decrease due to the decline in birth rate in China. Many vocational schools built to meet the previous educational needs of the school-aged population are likely to vanish in the long term. In order to achieve new breakthroughs, it is necessary to seek new development opportunities beyond vocational education and to adapt the function of vocational education. Therefore, vocational schools must reform in order to provide off-the-job training to enterprise employees and a lifelong learning service for the public. This transition is already in progress as we have discussed in previous chapters. Some schools have already completely transitioned to providing customised training programmes for enterprises and the public. In addition to vocational education for their own students, some schools provide general training or re-skilling to enterprises, particularly small- and medium-sized enterprises. Some schools also provide training to vocational teachers from other schools.

In terms of providing public training, vocational schools face problems such as institutional obstacles, insufficient funding and limited capacity to carry out tailor-made training programmes. For example, different demands from enterprises, lack of resource support, rigid school management systems and ineffective communication between stakeholders challenge the effective delivery of high-quality training programmes. Thus, the full potential of vocational schools needs to be explored and utilised in the future.

Ongoing exploration and innovation

The 'Self-Strengthening Movement' in China taking place in the second half of the 19th century provided opportunities for the development of China's modern VET which has been connected with the outside world from the outset. The initial vocational schools mainly taught modern science and technologies based on the Western education system. In the 1950s and 1960s, China's vocational education also learned from the former Soviet Union under the central planning system. Since China adopted its policy of reform and opening up to the outside world, the international exchanges and cooperation between China's vocational education and the outside world, mainly Western countries and Japan, have made many breakthroughs in both depth and scope.

The introduction of advanced foreign systems such as the German Dual System and the British Modern Apprenticeship and Japanese models played an active role in China's VET development. With the accumulation of experience, China's VET system has been transformed by a combination of foreign influences and

Chinese characteristics. In addition, with financial and equipment investments from foreign partners, the infrastructures of vocational schools have been significantly improved. Today, vocational schools have world-class equipment (e.g. computerised numerical control machine tools and car assembly equipment). With this technical support, new teaching philosophy (e.g. student-oriented) and methods (e.g. integration of knowledge and practice) have been adopted. The most up-to-date teaching materials are being offered to students and the overall learning experience of the students is being improved. Teachers have also gained the opportunity to attend training sessions held at the schools by international experts and/or go overseas for training. These factors have improved the overall quality of China's VET in a short period of time.

With the deepening of market economic reform, social transformation and expansion of enrolments at vocational schools, labour markets have also experienced rapid changes with increasing demand for a skilled workforce following the new national development focusing on 'innovative China' (State Council, 2018). This has led to a change in China's VET from emphasising content/connotation to placing greater importance on the improved quality of students' overall experience. The vocational schools are no longer run with reference to general education which focused on systematic subject knowledge. The vocational schools have gradually been opened up through efforts to deepen cross-border cooperation. Various concepts have emerged, such as school-enterprise cooperation, work-study combination, internship and placement, integration of knowledge and practice, and integration of production and education.

The aforementioned concepts have formed the basis for various experimental projects, such as enterprise-run vocational schools and school-run enterprises, educational group-run schools and industrial park-based vocational training centres. China's VET is actively promoting close cooperation at different levels with multiple stakeholders and striving to integrate production and education. According to the Report of National Secondary Vocational Schools' School-running Ability (Ministry of Education, 2016a), school-enterprise cooperation and work-study integration have become fundamental models for China's VET schools. A similar conclusion was drawn in the Report of Assessing National Tertiary Vocational Colleges Adaptation to Social Needs (Ministry of Education, 2016b) in the same year.

Therefore, integration between production and education and school-enterprise cooperation have achieved remarkable results. These developments are deeply embedded in China's economic transformation, and industrial and technological upgrading as one of the important elements of national economic development.

Future challenges and development directions

The increasing importance of secondary VET in China

For many years, Chinese society has placed higher value on the professions and white-collar jobs, while blue-collar work has been considered to have lower social status. It is not unusual to see Chinese parents want their children to pursue careers that will maintain or increase their social status and economic benefits. In terms of education, this preference is reflected in the value attributed to general academic education over vocational education. However, during our visit to vocational schools, some students confided that what they enjoyed doing most was working with their hands, whether on car engines, electrical circuits, hair or cosmetics, rather than studying abstract theory.

The necessity and importance of running secondary vocational education have been questioned and debated at various times in China. In the past, in order to improve the overall education level and achieve educational equity, China expanded the scale of its general academic education and reduced the scale of secondary vocational education or even suspended it. However, the 'Made in China 2025' strategy will allow manufacturing production and industrial infrastructure to undergo unprecedented changes (State Council, 2015). Human resources will face inevitable upgrading and optimisation, and a higher level of VET is expected to become the main vehicle for realising these goals. It is suggested that lower secondary school graduates should receive a general upper secondary school education, followed by a vocational education (State Council, 2016). Economically backward regions do not have the financial resources to develop VET, nor do they have the industrial foundation to support VET development. These limitations would suggest that these regions should focus on the development of their upper secondary school education, not secondary VET. However, it should be noted that there are over 280 million rural migrant workers (State Council, 2016) in China who require proper training to gain skills and employment opportunities. In addition, others, such as veterans, laid-off workers, and those with difficulties obtaining employment, also need training for re-skilling and upgrading skills in order to gain employment opportunities. Therefore, there is a great demand for vocational training and education, especially at secondary vocational level, in order to prepare these groups of people for new jobs.

VET and industrial transformation and upgrading

VET provides specific education and training in close association with industrial development. China's industries nowadays are under transformation and structural upgrading. A skilled workforce is the main force supporting the development of the advanced manufacturing industry and VET is the main channel for fostering a skilled workforce.

Traditional VET was established with the historical background of continuous development and the perfection of industrialisation. The educational purpose of VET is to promote practical technical talents that are compatible with standardised assembly line operations. A focus on technical training has suited requirements at specific times in history. In practice, vocational courses are often divided into disciplines according to the type of job/occupation and the content of the job/occupation. This skill training model is extremely practical, showing great superiority in the early stages of industrialisation. After graduation, students can quickly adapt to the working environment, meet job requirements, improve production efficiency and minimise costs. Moreover, the high employment rate of vocational graduates in this period has also made vocational education more attractive and has won praise for the development of vocational schools.

With the advancement of industrial transformation, industrial production has moved from traditional to innovative manufacturing. Resource-intensive and labour-intensive industries have gradually been phased out, and standardised and batch production has gradually been replaced by personalised and customised production. At the same time, the development of high-tech and service industries has been flourishing. These industries have created a strong demand for highly skilled workers. However, only one-third of Chinese industrial workers are skilled, 60% are junior-skilled workers, 35% are intermediate-skilled workers and 5% are senior-skilled workers (Pan, 2017). In Germany, senior-skilled workers account for 35–40% of the workforce (Xinhua, 2017). In addition, new technologies, models, designs and management systems and practices set higher requirements for the adaptability and comprehensive quality and skills of employees (e.g. professionalism, creativity, technical capability, teamwork, responsibility, loyalty and sense of safety).

In this sense, the employment-orientation characteristic of VET allows it to enjoy a first-mover advantage over general education. VET has a clear market demand orientation and is closely integrated with the development of industry and professional settings. By forming partnerships and designing customised training programmes with enterprises, VET shortens the occupational preparation time. By using teaching materials co-developed by the school and enterprises, VET fulfils the exact needs of enterprises for vocational skills. However, China's VET is always facing the challenge of how to reform further in order to meet market needs and better align itself with national development strategies.

VET and new urbanisation

In 2014, the Chinese Central Government issued a national plan promoting a new round of urbanisation (State Council, 2014b). Rather than focusing only on the expansion of existing large urban areas, the plan aimed to develop people-centred cities located in different parts of the country, including existing small towns, as part of a new urbanisation plan. Premier Li Keqiang declared in the government works report of 2016 that "the new urbanization promotes the highest potential to drive domestic consumption and growth" (State Council, 2016). Driven by labour migration, urbanisation has enabled China to meet the strong demand for labour across urban sectors.

The relation between urbanisation and VET is interactive. The urbanisation process has promoted the social division of labour and increased the demand for VET, which is conducive to the improvement of the scale, quality and efficiency of VET. The size of a city and its comprehensive strength determine the level (i.e. secondary or tertiary) and quantity of vocational education institutions. At the same time, the development of VET provides human resources for urbanisation, enhances urban economic and social competitiveness, improves the quality of employees, reduces poverty, accelerates labour mobility and urban-rural integration, and promotes the overall development of industries.

In addition, the degree of agricultural modernisation and the quality of farmers are important indicators of the level of urbanisation. With the further advancement of urbanisation, a large number of rural populations have become surplus labourers. They need to master a skill to settle in cities or return to agriculture as 'modern professional farmers' with advanced technology and skills. The case of VET07 described in the previous chapter demonstrates that VET has significant advantages in urbanisation and poverty alleviation.

Closer school-enterprise cooperation

There is consensus in the view that school-enterprise cooperation is an important feature of China's VET. In practice, the central government, local governments and schools promote cooperation between schools and enterprises in many ways. However, the current cooperation is widespread as it has been adopted by the majority of VET schools in China, but the depth of cooperation is low. The Eastern and Central regions enjoy a higher level of cooperation than the Western regions. In terms of industry-supported majors, medical and health, construction, information technology and manufacturing are better than education, business administration, art design, media, finance, business, tourism and agriculture.

Enterprises hope that vocational schools can meet their industry's skill needs, but also expect schools to provide technical services and staff training. Since the students graduating in certain regions and from certain schools are suitable for the needs of the enterprises, the cooperation between schools and enterprises is satisfactory. It is common practice for enterprises to donate equipment and provide funding and internship sites to support this cooperation. However, obstacles such as the costs incurred by enterprises engaging in cooperation cannot be compensated. In contrast, in Germany the cost of training is shared by enterprises and students (apprentices). The German government provides partial subsidies through the establishment of public technical schools and the promotion of compulsory vocational education. Industry associations and trade unions sign collective contracts through collective negotiation to guarantee the income and proper treatment of students (apprentices). This approach has largely solved the problem of enterprises being reluctant to invest in training and only wanting to recruit workers without investment.

Additionally, although great progress has been made in China, the research capabilities of vocational teachers and the contents of textbooks cannot keep up with the development needs of enterprises and industry, potentially leading to an imbalance in school-enterprise cooperation. With the impact of greater education popularisation, the imperfect vocational education system and the ineffective implementation of the national vocational qualification certificate system and labour access system, vocational school graduates may be in an unfavourable competitive position in the labour market. Therefore, the imbalance in school-enterprise cooperation is not only related to the inadequate and uneven industrial development among the different regions in China, but is also related to the curriculum framework setting, quality of training and service capacity among vocational schools. These issues need to be addressed as an important issue for future development.

Fostering of vocational teachers with 'dual certificate'

Many vocational schools in China, especially in rural areas, are experiencing a shortage of funding and infrastructure.

For example, the lack of 'dual certificate' teachers is manifested in two aspects, one is the lack of quantity and the other is the lack of quality. In August 2010, the Ministry of Education promulgated the standards for vocational schools. The number of teachers with senior professional and technical positions was to exceed 20% of the total number of teachers; the number of professional teachers was to be no less than 50% of the number of full-time teachers in the school, including more than 30% dual certificate teachers; each major was to be supported by at least two full-time teachers with relevant professional intermediates titles and above, and part-time teachers with practical experience were to account for approximately 20% of the total number of full-time teachers in the school (Ministry of Education, 2010).

Based on the education reform and development plan, the number of vocational students and graduates in China is expected to reach 38.3 million by 2020 (State Council, 2010). The continuous growth of vocational education and improvement in the quality of school operation require the support of sufficient dual certificate teachers. However, there is controversy in the definition of dual certificate teachers. At present, in many secondary vocational schools, a teacher who holds two certificates, namely a professional qualification (e.g. intermediate turner, advanced fitter or advanced metalworker) and a teacher qualification certificate, is defined as a dual certificate teacher. In fact, some teachers hold professional qualification certificates that are not compatible with the majors they teach. A number of teachers' professional qualification certificates are obtained through book study and examinations, and lack practical experience. Therefore, whether it is from the perspective of quantity or quality, the dual certificate system within VET needs much improvement.

Building vocational training bases

In addition to the lack of dual certificate teachers, not all vocational schools in China can provide sufficient training space for students. In the VET system, there are three main types of training bases, namely the on-campus training base, the enterprise training base and the public training base. The on-campus training base is a factory/production unit built in the school for students to practice their internships, with the school being the main platform for such practice. The enterprise training base is a factory/production unit established within the enterprise for the apprentices to simulate real situations, and the enterprise is the main platform. The public training base consists of a wide range of training facilities and targets a variety of institutions, enterprises, training centres and social groups. All these training bases are insufficient in terms of quantity. Furthermore, training bases in vocational schools can only provide students with basic vocational skills and scenario simulations. Enterprises rarely take the initiative to establish an enterprise training base and cooperate with the schools because of concerns related to the cost. Enterprises prefer students to be exposed to the actual work environment in the company in order to practice, thus saving on costs. However, without proper training for students on operational procedures and operation norms before working in an actual work environment, the training process may not be efficient and results unsatisfactory. Training bases guaranteeing sufficient quantity and effectiveness are one of the determinants of the overall quality of students. The government's support and the cooperation between enterprises and schools are essential in solving these challenges.

Promotion of students' professionalism

China's industries have experienced remarkable growth since the start of reform and opening up. However, the size of the industries does not necessarily guarantee their strength. Considering China's transition from high-speed to high-quality growth, professionalism has become more important than ever. Initially, professionalism was narrowly defined as craftsmanship, referring to the pursuit of perfection. Gradually meticulous attention to detail at work was incorporated in this definition, finally including also the ability to innovate in order to keep abreast of the times. Throughout the history of industrialisation, craftsmanship has been an indispensable aspect of every innovation that has led to major industrial transformation.

In the context of VET, the concept of professionalism is widely used. Besides the key component of craftsmanship, professionalism includes ability and professional attitude, incorporating persistence, loyalty and responsibility (State Council, 2019). These attributes form the core spirit of professional fields and constitute an important guarantee for the country's long-term development. VET is at the forefront of the cultivation of a skilled workforce in manufacturing. In order to meet the needs of modern production development, the Ministry of Education issued a number of documents on the comprehensive improvement of the quality of VET as early as 2006 (Ministry of Education, 2006). These documents outlined three elements for high-quality technical and skilled talent: professional ability (including vocational skills and professional qualities), workplace ability (including the ability to take responsibility in the workplace) and innovation and problem-solving skills. China's vocational schools have vigorously applied these principles of professionalism. In the future, it is expected that schools and enterprises, as well as teachers and mentors, will jointly train students and transform the traditional linear education and training relationship into a multifaceted education model.

Students' career management

Career preparation and planning is a compulsory course for every vocational student, as ordered by China's Ministry of Education. Leaving aside the question of whether this is the best way to conduct career management through classroom teaching, the move reflects the importance given to career management. However, it is always a challenge for secondary vocational students to enter a workplace at a young age and compete with students who are three or four years older with higher academic qualification. Hence, preparing and planning a career path is a meaningful issue for both schools and students.

Each year many students are not able to reach the required score in the upper secondary school entrance exam. Some choose to go to secondary vocational schools. Faced with the many majors offered by secondary vocational schools, many students and parents often prefer to choose the majors which 'sound good' or can help find jobs easily, or make random choices of majors. In these cases, there is no in-depth understanding and clear cognition of the major or how the students will be trained in relation to employment after graduation. After entering the school, some students lack the motivation to study, immersing themselves in the pessimistic emotions arising from failure in entrance examinations. These students have a strong sense of defeat and inferiority, making the learning process difficult and painful. After graduation, secondary vocational graduates are mostly engaged in the first line of production and service. With insufficient workplace experience, some of them are not able to fit in the workplace environment which could be trivial, complicated and unpredictable. Once the exciting period of being a 'rookie' in the workplace has passed, the graduates can easily become tired of repetitive routine work and have problems of workplace burnout. Some graduates may reach their limits for further promotion due to their limited academic qualifications, resulting in confusion and frequent changes of jobs and employers.

In order to address this problem, many projects have been launched for tackling vocational students' career development. However, as we discussed earlier, the preference for academic excellence prevails over skills. Parents do not consciously create an environment suitable for students' vocational awareness or provide career-oriented values and guidance, resulting in a lack of knowledge of the majors offered by schools. Students' social cognitions are also poorly developed; they are unclear about their own advantages and disadvantages, do not form good professional concepts and judgements, and show a lack of awareness of career planning and career management skills. Many vocational schools offer career education, subject to the requirements of the government agencies rather than the actual needs of students' career development. At present, the most common way of conducting career management is based on classroom teaching without much practical input. The course evaluation is also based on a written test or report. Career counselling for graduates is underdeveloped in China. There is a lack of professional and specialised consulting organisations or personnel to assist graduates who are confused about their career development.

The agenda for future reforms

One of the Chinese government's objectives is to ensure that by the middle of this century, China will become an all-round well-off society. To this end, a new avenue to industrialisation is to be taken to speed up urbanisation and innovative economic development. At the same time, the requirements for skills related to new employment and re-employment needs are to be increased, and educational, scientific and cultural undertakings are to be enhanced. Further efforts will be made to develop VET and quicken the pace of HRD so as to transform the large population in China into advanced human capital. Although impressive progress has been achieved, greater efforts are needed to deepen the reform of China's VET and the following agenda highlighted by the governments and followed by VET schools reflects the future development direction.

First, given the characteristics of China's VET, its reform is aligned with national development strategies such as 'Made in China 2025', transforming from 'Made in China' to 'Innovated in China' and the new urbanisation plan. To reinforce VET's contribution to overall development, vocational schools need to be adjusted according to the new professional development plan and relevant new majors are timeously needed. VET schools also need to pay more attention to the cultivation of soft skills such as communication and professionalism (e.g. sprit of craftsmanship). Furthermore, the schools need to continue to strengthen resource sharing and promote the deep integration of production and education as well as actively participate in providing training to improve the skills of current employees in enterprises. With regard to the development of new urbanisation, vocational schools, especially those located in rural areas, have a significant advantage in facilitating the transition to urbanisation. Central and local governments need to increase their support for vocational education in poverty-stricken areas.

Second, China's VET system has achieved a relatively developed status compared to its initial stage. However, achieving integration between different education sectors at all levels is a key measure to promote the smooth operation of the modern VET system. In order to open up the channels for educational transition between different levels of vocational education, between different types of vocational education, and between vocational education and general education, it is necessary to build a modern vocational education system that includes credit recognition, curriculum integration, certificate exchange, self-regulated admission examination, flexible learning and resource integration. From the perspective of promoting the linkages of contents between vocational education and general education, it is necessary to strengthen vocational education in primary and secondary schools, enrich the content and form of students' professional experience, and establish a career planning and guidance system throughout the individual's learning and career development process.

Third, to fully utilise the function of vocational schools in meeting diversified needs, vocational schools in China will continue to develop the simultaneous development of degree-based vocational education and non-degree-based vocational education (e.g. general training for the public, and tailor-made training for enterprises). Authority should be further devolved to vocational schools in order to encourage them to be more market-driven and more involved in utilising other resources from industries and enterprises. VET schools should provide learners with a variety of learning experiences and methods, study time and learning curriculum choices in order to build a society with highly a skilled workforce.

Fourth, in order to solve the inadequate and imbalanced school-enterprise cooperation, China's vocational education needs to establish a long-term mechanism for school-enterprise cooperation. As a first step, it should clarify the responsibilities of the various stakeholders (government, school, enterprise and other relevant stakeholders) and then restructure their responsibilities to establish a common governance model, including industry standards, schools' responsibility for training and government supervision of the operation. By drawing on the experience of Germany and Japan, China's VET should give enterprises a more important role to play in terms of facilitating the development of schools, and this should be regulated by national legislation. There are existing school-enterprise cooperation policies and legislation established by both the central and local governments; some policies and regulations have been implemented for several years but have not been able to achieve the expected outcomes. Therefore, during the next round of new legislation, it is necessary to conduct an analysis and evaluation to identify the gaps and form more effective national legislation.

Furthermore, legislation should focus on the details of cooperation, such as the necessary qualifications of the cooperating enterprise and its practical instructors, the objectives, contents, forms, time, duration and assessment of the cooperative education programmes. The obligations of the enterprises to the students should also be stipulated, including the obligation to pay for the internships and the obligation of acceptance of agency supervision and the legal responsibility for breaching vocational education obligations. It is also necessary to give enterprises the same legal status as the vocational education providers in order for them to play an adequate role in the process of cooperation with vocational schools. The government policy of tax reduction, financial support and other incentives can also encourage enterprises to participate and contribute to a greater extent in vocational education. Since China's laws and policies are more principled and instructive with a relatively low implement ability, lessons should be drawn from other countries' experiences, such as Germany, where school-enterprise cooperation is regulated with very detailed stipulations and are highly operational.

Fifth, China should continue the development of a national VET qualification framework. The importance of developing the framework is three-fold: (1) the qualifications within the framework are divided into gradual progressive levels, which provide the premise for a grading system basis for vocational education courses; (2) the qualifications within the framework are based on the criteria for learning outcomes, which reflect the actual improvement in acquiring knowledge and skills; (3) the qualifications of different levels within the national qualification framework also correspond to the professional competence requirements at different levels, and this also reflects the career development requirements as a crucial part of vocational education.

Given that the development of a national VET qualification framework involves multiple stakeholders, including education administration departments, teaching and research institutions, vocational schools and industrial enterprises, it is necessary to establish a four-party coordination mechanism to develop the framework.

Sixth, quality education is vital to the future of China's VET and requires an appropriate quality assurance system which can be divided into an external and internal system. With regard to the external quality assurance system, China could draw on the educational quality assurance system in Germany and Japan by: (1) establishing a specialised vocational education quality assessment institution; (2) giving the industry an important role to evaluate the quality of vocational education; (3) strengthening the legislation on vocational education; (4) improving the government's capital investment mechanism with incentives. As for the internal quality assurance system, China could adopt an internal auditing mechanism, curriculum quality assurance system, vocational education teacher qualification assessment system and a vocational education quality feedback system as the UK has previously done.

Seventh, evaluation of educational quality is another long-lasting challenge faced by China's VET. In Germany, the UK and Japan, third-party evaluation has become the norm and procedural routine for educational evaluation. In China, so far, third-party involvement has faced many problems such as unclear rights and responsibilities, unqualified industry access to qualifications and standards, insufficient supervision and management mechanisms. To solve these problems, it is necessary to improve relevant laws and regulations to clarify third-party rights and responsibilities, provide legal protection for third-party evaluations, formulate and improve industry norms, establish and improve credit evaluation mechanisms for third-party organisations, and provide incentive policies for the development of third-party institutions.

Eighth, career management requires cooperation between families, schools and the public. Vocational schools could organise workshops during enrolment sessions to explain the characteristics of the various majors, training plans, course contents and the most recent needs of the job market. During the annual vocational education week held by the government, schools could showcase their teaching results. Thus, students and their parents could have a clear understanding of the majors before entering the vocational school. In addition, it is meaningful to establish a student-oriented career education concept by focusing on meeting students' expectations and long-term career needs with adequate actions such as reconstructing the career curriculum system, reforming career teaching methods and enhancing the quality of career teachers in vocational schools. By developing schools' career management systems, the schools can collect relevant career information to build career profiles for students until their graduation. Relevant information, such as students' career interests, skills qualifications, internships and placement experiences, can be used for further career counselling and follow-up service.

Implications for HRD

During the past decades, considerable attention has been paid to VET in China. Being one of the pillars for economic and industrial development, VET has trained a great number of skilled workforces for industries in general and enterprises in manufacturing sector in particular. VET graduates have been trained with practical skills and are capable of working at the first line of production in enterprises immediately after graduation. The graduates have basic knowledge which provides a possibility for further study.

From the perspective of HRD, China's VET currently still faces the problem of providing complete and systematic ongoing training and career guidance for students. This situation potentially leads to issues such as high turnover rate of VET graduates due to the mismatch between the training programmes provided in the schools and the skills and quality required in the labour markets. For enterprises, the high turnover rate significantly increases labour costs, and for individual VET graduates, jumping between different employers and jobs is an unpleasant process. In this sense, creating more training opportunities and providing adequate career counselling services may be feasible solutions to these issues and may largely increase the quality and stability of VET graduates. Consequently, a sufficient supply of high-quality VET graduates contributes to a more reasonable and balanced structure of the workforce, which is critical to China's economic and industrial development.

Economic and industrial development processes have a significant impact on HRD policies. As China's industrial structure upgrades, it requires corresponding changes and improvements in skills development among the workforce and related HRD policies. For example, as a foundation industry, the manufacturing sector needs a great number of skilled workers at intermediate and advanced levels in both the short term and the long term. Reflected in the design and implementation of HRD and VET policies, the aims are to build a capable workforce in the short term and develop sustainable HRD and VET systems in the long term. As for the newly emerged sectors, such as artificial intelligence, big data and 3D-print, the VET policies and practices at school level focus on ongoing updating knowledge in order to meet the needs of industry development and seize the relevant opportunities. Therefore, the balanced and coordinated development of HRD and VET policies could advance the transitional economy in China with meaningful implications for other countries at a similar level of economic development.

In the early stages of development, most transitional economies lack many advantages such as capital investment, managerial experience, know-how, advanced technology and training methods. As seen in China's case, governments at different levels play an important role which changes along the development process for better facilitation of overall progress. Initially, governments can be the main promoters, governing bodies and main providers of financial and technical assistance to HRD in general and VET in particular. Governments' determination to develop HRD and VET is vital. Gradually, governments need to be the coordinators in managing other stakeholders, especially industries, enterprises and schools, and allocating and managing resources accordingly. The participation of industries and enterprises needs to be encouraged and rewarded by governments. The release of a certain amount of managerial power allows the schools to also gain more autonomy in a number of ways. In the future, the participation of industries and enterprises needs to be reinforced further. Only with the proactive participation of these two entities will the HRD system, especially VET, be able to foster graduates whose skills, abilities and characteristics (e.g. working attitude and work morality) fulfil the needs at the workplace. Industries and enterprises should be the main providers of support to HRD and VET, while governments should play the role of supervisors and resource coordinators.

Well-established HRD and VET models provide valuable experience to other transitional economies who intend to develop their own HRD and VET models. China learned from Germany, Britain and Japan as well as other countries, achieving a significant increase in the quality of VET graduates and the workforce. The country has gradually moved to modify these models in order to enhance alignment with regional and local conditions and needs. With a successful modification, these models have been adapted to the Chinese context and promoted from coastal areas to inland areas. By collecting feedback from both coastal and inland areas, the already-modified HRD and VET models enter another round of refining. The process repeats in an upward spiral.

It appears that transitional economies have to deal with many difficulties and problems, but they enjoy certain advantages. For example, these economies can take a shortcut in adopting the newest HRD and VET models without a heavy burden from the past. In addition, by examining the existing models from other countries, these economies do not have to limit themselves to a particular model; they can enjoy a high level of flexibility to choose, combine and optimise. Furthermore, during the process of developing new systems, stakeholders normally undertake strong initiatives to make changes, which can be reflected in favourable new legislation regarding the development of HRD and VET, strong determination from government across all levels to support the development, strong motivation from school management to innovate, and a high level of participation from teachers and students during the reform process. In this sense, transitional economies should embrace these special characteristics and fully utilise their advantages to accelerate the pace of development in HRD and VET.

Conclusion

Conducting HRD studies in transitional economies is difficult in the initial stages because many countries such as China have not formulated systematic and specific policies and practices for HRD in general, VET in particular.

In China, many experimental practices have been undertaken along the way of development.

Based on the reviews and cases in previous chapters, this book has shown that China does not have a single VET model which can be applied nationwide. With some basic patterns in organising VET, a number of central themes have emerged such as matching skills between the needs of markets and VET training programmes, and combining production and education through integration between theories and practices with a focus on 6- to 12-month internships and replacement before graduation. In contrast to the adoption of well-established VET models, these patterns take Chinese contextual issues into considerations such as uneven economic development between different regions, a large rural population, relatively insufficient investment in VET, and unclear division of authority in VET. In other words, China's VET has borrowed ideas and models from advanced economies, and at the same time, is implementing these with national, regional and local characteristics. It is too early to conclude whether a single VET model is superior to the diversified models given the size and national characteristics of China.

China is on a fast track to modernisation and deepened marketisation, and needs a great number of high-quality workforces. The new generations should be well trained with practical skills, positive working attitudes and a certain degree of possibilities for further learning. Being important players in cultivating skilled workforces, more attention and investment from policymakers, educators, industries, enterprises, teachers and students are required. It is reasonable to believe that the quality of workforce will affect China's development significantly. In terms of HRD in general, and the development of VET in particular, the journey towards the future will be long but eventually fruitful.

References

Ministry of Education, 2006. Several opinions of the Ministry of Education on improving the teaching quality of higher vocational education [online] http://www.moe.gov.cn Available at http://www.moe.gov.cn/srcsite/A07/s7055/200611/t20061116_79649.html [accessed on 20 February 2018]

Ministry of Education, 2010. Secondary vocational education reform and innovation action plan [online] http://www.moe.gov.cn Available at http://www.moe.gov.cn/srcsite/A07/s7055/201011/t20101127_171574.html [accessed on 8 February 2018]

Ministry of Education, 2016a. The report of national secondary vocational schools' school-running ability [online] http://www.moe.gov.cn Available at http://www.moe.gov.cn/s78/A07/moe_731/201712/t20171207_320820.html [accessed on 30 December 2018]

Ministry of Education, 2016b. The report of assessing national tertiary vocational colleges' adaptation to social needs [online] http://www.moe.gov.cn Available at http://www.moe.gov.cn/srcsite/A11/moe_764/201603/t20160323_234947.html [accessed on 30 December 2018]

Pan, C. G. 2017. *Annual report on the development of Chinese talents 2017.* Beijing: Social Sciences Academic Press.

State Council, 2010. Outline of national medium- and long-term education reform and development plan (2010–2020) [online] http://www.gov.cn/index.htm Available at http://www.gov.cn/jrzg/2010-07/29/content_1667143.htm [accessed on 18 February 2019]

State Council, 2014a. National new urbanisation plan (2014–2020) [online] http://www.gov.cn/index.htm Available at http://www.gov.cn/zhengce/content/2014-06/22/content_8901.htm [accessed on 9 January 2018]

State Council, 2014b. National new urbanisation plan (2014–2020) [online] http://www.gov.cn/index.htm Available at http://www.gov.cn/gongbao/content/2014/content_2644805.htm [accessed on 16 January 2018]

State Council, 2015. Made in China 2025 [online] http://www.gov.cn/index.htm Available at http://www.gov.cn/zhengce/content/2015-05/19/content_9784.htm [accessed on 12 January 2018]

State Council, 2016. National government work report [online] http://www.gov.cn/index.htm Available at http://www.gov.cn/guowuyuan/2016-03/17/content_5054901.htm [accessed on 10 February 2019]

State Council, 2018. The State Council's opinion on promoting the high-quality development of innovation and entrepreneurship to create an upgraded version of "double innovation" [online] http://www.gov.cn/index.htm Available at http://www.gov.cn/zhengce/content/2018-09/26/content_5325472.htm [accessed on 14 February 2019]

State Council, 2019. National vocational education reform implementation plan [online] http://www.gov.cn/index.htm Available at http://www.gov.cn/zhengce/content/2019-02/13/content_5365341.htm [accessed on 19 February 2019]

The National People's Congress of the People's Republic China, 1996. [online] http://www.npc.gov.cn Available at http://www.npc.gov.cn/npc/zfjc/zfjcelys/2015-06/28/content_1939676.htm [accessed on 30 December 2018]

Xinhua, 2017. Where is the 'big country craftsman'? The gap between China's senior technicians is as high as 10 million. [online] http://www.xinhuanet.com Available at http://www.xinhuanet.com//2017-04/17/c_1120820859.htm [accessed on 21 January 2018]

Index

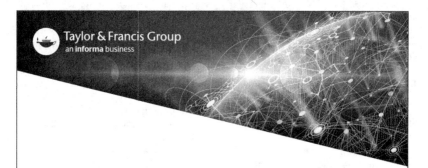

Printed in the United States
by Baker & Taylor Publisher Services